Measuring Student Development

Gary R. Hanson, *Editor*

NEW DIRECTIONS FOR STUDENT SERVICES
URSULA DELWORTH and GARY R. HANSON, *Editors-in-Chief*

Number 20, December 1982

Paperback sourcebooks in
The Jossey-Bass Higher Education Series

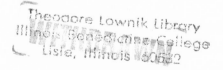

Jossey-Bass Inc., Publishers
San Francisco • Washington • London

Gary R. Hanson (Ed.).
Measuring Student Development.
New Directions for Student Services, no. 20.
San Francisco: Jossey-Bass, 1982.

New Directions for Student Services Series
Ursula Delworth and Gary R. Hanson, *Editors-in-Chief*

New Directions for Student Services (publication number USPS
449-070) is published quarterly by Jossey-Bass Inc., Publishers.
Second-class postage rates paid at San Francisco, California,
and at additional mailing offices.

Correspondence:
Subscriptions, single-issue orders, change of address notices,
undelivered copies, and other correspondence should be sent to
New Directions Subscriptions, Jossey-Bass Inc., Publishers,
433 California Street, San Francisco, California 94104.

Editorial correspondence should be sent to the Editors-in-Chief,
Ursula Delworth, University Counseling Service, Iowa
Memorial Union, University of Iowa, Iowa City, Iowa 52242
or Gary R. Hanson, Office of the Dean of Students,
Student Services Building, Room 101, University of Texas
at Austin, Austin, Texas 78712.

Library of Congress Catalogue Card Number LC 81-48582

International Standard Serial Number ISSN 0164-7970

International Standard Book Number ISBN 87589-922-6

Cover art by Willi Baum

Manufactured in the United States of America

Ordering Information

The paperback sourcebooks listed below are published quarterly and can be ordered either by subscription or as single copies.

Subscriptions cost $35.00 per year for institutions, agencies, and libraries. Individuals can subscribe at the special rate of $21.00 per year *if payment is by personal check.* (Note that the full rate of $35.00 applies if payment is by institutional check, even if the subscription is designated for an individual.) Standing orders are accepted.

Single copies are available at $7.95 when payment accompanies order, and *all single-copy orders under $25.00 must include payment.* (California, Washington, D.C., New Jersey, and New York residents please include appropriate sales tax.) For billed orders, cost per copy is $7.95 plus postage and handling. (Prices subject to change without notice.)

To ensure correct and prompt delivery, all orders must give either the *name of an individual* or an *official purchase order number.* Please submit your order as follows:

Subscriptions: specify series and subscription year.
Single Copies: specify sourcebook code and issue number (such as, SS8).

Mail orders for United States and Possessions, Latin America, Canada, Japan, Australia, and New Zealand to:
Jossey-Bass Inc., Publishers
433 California Street
San Francisco, California 94104

Mail orders for all other parts of the world to:
Jossey-Bass Limited
28 Banner Street
London EC1Y 8QE

New Directions for Student Services Series
Ursula Delworth and Gary R. Hanson, *Editors-in-Chief*

Contents

Editor's Notes

She looked at her shoes mostly and wondered why she had let herself get cornered by the dean on her very first day of college. She didn't want to talk to the dean in the first place, and attending all of the orientation meetings made her uncomfortable anyway. Now, she had to think of something to say. Maybe the dean knew something about that special section of honors English. He at least ought to know where her dormitory was located. So they talked, but only briefly. She was shy, a long way from home, and all too relieved to get out the nearest door. Was college going to be like this all the time?

Five years later Sue hailed the dean from across the campus and came running up barely able to contain her excitement. She had a job. She described with great animation her anxious moments waiting to hear she had been hired. But what she really wanted to tell him was what an important part he had played in her college life. He had listened a lot, but, more than that he had cared who she was. She had changed and they both know it. She wasn't shy, loved to discuss current events, and had been an active campus leader during her last two years. She felt confident of her many new skills and couldn't wait to try them out in her new job. And she didn't watch her shoes anymore.

If you work with students at all, you know they change. They grow up. They think and behave differently. And you wonder how and why it happens. Students like Sue will tell you that YOU made a difference. College made a difference. Deep down you hope it's true.

I hope you wonder how and why students develop the way they do. We can't be very intentional about what we do if we do not at least ask questions about how students change. More importantly, we have a mandate to find the answers. Our professional reputations are on the line. Our philosophical history provides us with the rationale for why we must be interested, and our theory guides our thinking so we can make some educated guesses as to the how, when, and why of student development. We simply will never know unless we can document that students change as a result of what we do. We have to measure student development to understand, influence, and document how they change. Without the documentation we cease to be either very intentional or very effective.

The purpose of this volume is to examine what we know about the measurement of student development. In the chapters that follow,

1

we will ask why we measure student development at all, what we should be measuring, and some reasons why it is so difficult to capture how students change in college. A review of available assessment instruments will be provided to aid the interested professional in selecting the best possible instrument for a particular use. Finally, a case study of how a student development program used assessment results for programming purposes is provided.

In Chapter One, Theodore K. Miller reminds us why the assessment of student development is important. He provides a historical and philosophical overview of how the concepts of student development came to be embraced by our institutions of higher education. The rationale for why student affairs practitioners should pursue a developmental approach in the delivery of their student services is provided. Miller sees the assessment of student development as the "glue" that holds the developmental process together. The assessment of student development not only provides information to the individual and the institution but also encourages and facilitates the development of students. Miller also urges that the student affairs professional acquire good assessment skills in order that the development of students occur in a purposeful and planned manner, one not to be left to chance factors.

In Chapter Two, Karen Kitchener discusses the *what* of student development. Knowing what aspects of student development to assess is difficult because of the many complex theories and models of student development. In this chapter, two general models of student development are discussed; one deals with the process and structure regarding the ways in which students learn to think and the second deals with the developmental tasks required of college students today. Both models have important implications for what we ought to be measuring about students. The implication for the assessment of student development is particularly important because, as Kitchener points out, the social-cognitive development of students is not completed during their undergraduate college years, yet college students are faced with specific developmental tasks that require very complex decision making. As a consequence, students are placed in a developmental double bind.

Very little assessment of student development is taking place on today's college campuses. A wide variety of reasons prevents both faculty and student affairs professionals from taking an active role in the assessment process. In the third chapter, Gary R. Hanson discusses the critical issues that form barriers to the assessment process. Some of the issues involve the politics of assessment and some, the fact that few student affairs professionals have adequate training in the development, administration, and interpretation of student development assessment devices. A discussion of these critical issues is provided in order to help student services professionals become more involved in the assessment of student development in an active and intentional way.

Another reason very little assessment of student development seems to be occurring is that few people know very much about the available assessment instruments. The assessment of student development can either be formal or informal, and Robert Mines, in Chapter Four, reviews many of the formal assessment instruments. He discusses a number of available assessment formats for measuring development and highlights some of the issues involving the administration, scoring, and interpretation of the instruments. He also provides an evaluation and critique of their psychometric quality.

Relatively few individuals have the opportunity to design a student service program that includes rigorous and systematic assessment of the ways students change as a result of participating in the program. In the fifth chapter, Kathleen J. Krone and Gary R. Hanson describe the design, implementation, and evaluation of a residence hall program to facilitate the development of the residents in some very systematic ways. The ways in which the assessment process influenced various aspects of the day-to-day delivery of the program will be examined. A case study approach is used to help others avoid some of the pitfalls of the student assessment process and to capitalize on the things that worked well.

Finally, in the concluding remarks section I try to take a look at where we now stand and to anticipate where we might be going. The assessment of how students develop and change has been influenced by a proliferation of theoretical and conceptual models, but only recently have good, sound assessment techniques been developed. The difficult and time-consuming nature of our current methods should not restrict our efforts; rather, we should be encouraged that what we have accomplished so far provides a good foundation for doing an even better job in the future. The last section of this chapter will include some important references to help the interested professional learn more about what to assess, how to assess, where to look for available instruments, and where to find other important articles and book chapters on the student development assessment process.

Gary R. Hanson
Editor

Gary R. Hanson is assistant dean of students at the University of Texas at Austin and is responsible for the student life studies area of the Office of the Dean of Students.

The assessment of student development serves many purposes,
and the student services professional must understand the
historical and philosophical background of the developmental
perspective, recognize the role assessment plays in development,
and develop the skills needed to conduct good assessment.

Student Development Assessment: A Rationale

Theodore K. Miller

The uniqueness of higher education in America is reflected in its relationship to the larger society within which it flourishes. As the concept of the democratic society has expanded, the role, function, and complexity of postsecondary education has changed. American higher education has not developed in a vacuum, but has been generated by the American dream as much as any other social institution. As a result, students influenced and educated during the past 350 years have received much of the same nourishment and many of the same challenges as has the nation in general. American society has lavished much upon its educational enterprises, and they, in turn, have produced many generations of contributors, leaders, and innovators. Society is, to a certain extent, a result of its educational system as much as the system is a result of the society. The symbiotic relationships that exist between citizens and higher education institutions are very important, and both educational and political leaders need to take them into account as they strive to strengthen both the institutions and the nation. Assessment plays a special role in this overall process.

Historical and Philosophical Perspectives

The deliberate development of students has been and continues to be a primary function of the higher education enterprise. Definitions

G. R. Hanson (Ed.). *Measuring Student Development.* New Directions
for Student Services, no. 20. San Francisco: Jossey-Bass, December 1982.

of that development, its forms, processes, and preferred outcomes, however, have changed numerous times over the years. Every historical era has had an impact upon how the citizens of the day viewed the role and function of higher education, to what extent and in what ways they would support it, and the expectations they placed upon these important social institutions to carry out their bidding.

In the beginning, even though the colonial institutions were funded by public monies and governed by public trustees (Herbst, 1974), religious objectives dominated their existence and promoted cohesive and unified approaches. The very nature of early educational approaches led rapidly to what has come to be called the collegiate way of life (Brubacher and Rudy, 1976; Leonard, 1956; Rudolph, 1962), wherein students were viewed by those in charge as in need of close supervision and control in all areas of their lives by those in charge. The philosophy that prevailed was paternalistic, and the desired developmental outcomes were spiritual, moral, and vocational as much as they were intellectual. By connecting the supervisory role directly to all aspects of a student's life it was possible for institutions to reflect much of what had been the young person's family's responsibility in earlier times and other places (Leonard, 1956). In their own way, and unsophisticated as they may have been, the earliest American colleges were actually very much concerned about developing the student as a whole person.

As time passed, a new nation emerged, bringing with it new societal values, purposes, and perspectives. Elitist norms were eroded by the egalitarian and utilitarian principles that accompanied Jacksonian democracy in the mid-nineteenth century. Students responded to attempts to conserve and enhance the classical course of study by demanding diversity and creating literary societies, social clubs, and Greek-name fraternities. At the same time, women's education in the form of coeducational and single-sex institutions was begun. Federal legislation such as the Morrill Act of 1862 established land-grant colleges with emphasis upon a technical and applied education that challenged even more the classical and formalistic traditions so long in evidence. By the time the new republic was a century old, the industrial revolution was unfolding and the United States was moving rapidly from an agrarian to an industrial nation. Not only were the changes extensive, they were also occurring more rapidly. The country was moving to higher levels of complexity, as were the institutions of higher learning.

Coupled with the social and industrial changes were the responsive educational changes. Travel times were becoming shorter and communications were expanding. Intellectual intercourse with Europe was increasing, and concepts of academic freedom, intellectualism, and research were impacting American higher education. Many institutions increased their emphasis upon students' intellects, while the students increasingly became responsible for their own spiritual, social, and cultural life and welfare. By the beginnings of the twentieth century, the once unified and largely integrated academic and extracurricular elements of student life had become separate, distinct, and increasingly unrelated. In response, many educational institutions made something of a concerted effort to confront this perceived threat to the academic enterprise. Attempts were made to reinstitutionalize the students' extracurricular life by reintegrating it with the curriculum (Brubacher and Rudy, 1976). Whereas for many years the institutional leaders had taken largely a liberal approach to student development of all but the intellectual, the pendulum is swinging back to the earlier view that the students' total life experience was educational and therefore worthy of institutional attention. This time, however, it was not the clerically dominated faculty that was assigned to respond but, rather, persons who held a newly created position — the student personnel officer (Findley, 1939). The result was the student personnel movement.

Once again, programs of higher learning sought to attend to the needs of students in more holistic ways. The advent of the vocational guidance and testing movements manifested this renewed concern for the whole student. Increasingly, student support programs, such as campus-supervised housing, student health services, student unions and activities, vocational counseling, and placement offices, were coming into existence. The increased complexity in both society and postsecondary education required new and innovative approaches to working with college students, and there was an increasing concern for students' extracurricular life and related experiences. There was also evidence of a growing divergence in the philosophical positions taken by those responsible for implementing the student personnel programs, processes, and procedures. By the midpoint of the twentieth century, there were numerous schools of thought in evidence about how best to work with students. One position was exemplified by the belief that students were young and inexperienced and that the legal concept of *in loco parentis* should dominate, creating a paternalistic relationship between students and institutions. Another position was represented by the continued belief that it was not the institution's concern what students did outside the classroom. Between these extremes was a growing view that students were more nearly adults than children and that they must learn to be responsible by having opportunities to practice responsible behavior within the educational environment. This latter viewpoint represented a middle ground approach that encouraged both permissiveness and strong institutional support and was based upon the best thinking of the day, probably best expressed in *The Student Personnel Point of View*

(American Council on Education, 1937, 1949). After some 300 years, the developmental cycles had carried American higher education to a point of readiness to again address students' education and development on a more holistic basis.

What student affairs practice needed most by the third quarter of the twentieth century was a theoretical framework to complement its philosophical presuppositions and guide practice so that students would benefit as whole persons. Whereas the college students of the 1950s were generally quiet and passive, on most campuses the students of the 1960s were much more vocal and active, in many instances demanding that institutions change their response patterns to better recognize student needs. Such activist and sometimes violent behavior stimulated college administrations to seek solutions. To their credit, many institutions sought to respond to student concerns on the basis of adult-to-adult relationships, rather than on parent-to-child ones. This reflected the fact that students were increasingly being viewed as adults, were expected to behave as adults, and were required to experience the consequences of their behavior as adults. Obviously, this called for new ways of dealing with students. Although the general developmental outcomes expected from students' educational experiences were not radically altered, the processes and procedures for accomplishing them were. The advent in the 1960s and 1970s of human development theories applicable to college students was something of a boon to institutions of higher learning. Concepts underlying the processes of development formed a viable theoretical foundation upon which to build. In effect, the application of human development theory to student affairs practice initiated the student development movement in higher education.

Human development theory has practically exploded upon the college scene during the past few decades. From the seminal writings of theoreticians such as Erikson (1963), Havighurst (1953), Piaget (1952), and Lewin (1936) have come research, application models, intervention strategies, and expanded theoretical principles and approaches with direct implications for work with college students. The works of Sanford (1967), Chickering (1969), Heath (1968), Perry (1970), Kohlberg (1969), and Moos (1973), among others, have in various forms built on developmental theory to study and propose alternative approaches for work with college students. Student development, defined as the application of human development theory to work with students, has had a great impact upon institutions of higher learning in a relatively short period of time. Whether or not this theoretical foundation will alter the form of higher education in years to come is yet to be determined. Its presence, however, has already had much influence and seems to be generating ever new and different processes and procedures for facilitating the development and growth of college students. Student affairs practitioners cannot afford to overlook the importance of this theory and its underlying principles to the field in general and to work with students in particular.

Why Developmental Approaches?

Student affairs practitioners have a unique opportunity to aid in achieving the mission of higher education as it relates to the growth, development, and education of whole students. Student affairs practice has been in transition almost from its inception. This transitional process has influenced how practitioners view their primary purposes, responsibilities, and approaches as well as how they have structured their organizations and environments. As student affairs practice becomes more effective and practitioners become more skilled and professional, increasing numbers of faculty members and administrators come to see student affairs programs as being parallel to formal instruction as an essential part of the overall educational process (Wrenn, 1968). Those responsible for creating and maintaining the cocurricular aspects of students' educational experiences have great potential for facilitating the integration of the many important elements needed to make student development a reality.

In many ways it has been the student affairs practitioner who has carried the torch for total student development as an accepted and legitimate mission of higher education, often in direct opposition to others in the academic community. For instance, although the Carnegie Commission's analysis of higher education in the early 1970s evidenced a felt need on the part of students for institutions to attend to their total development, the commission report contended that it was neither wise nor possible to take direct responsibility for the total development of students, because that responsibility belongs to the individual student (Carnegie Commission, 1973). The report, however, did note that "the primary direct responsibility of the college is to assist with intellectual and skill development" (p. 16), which implies that such elements can and should be intentionally separated from total student development. On the one hand, the statement says that institutions should not take direct responsibility for development of the whole person, while on the other it indicates that institutions should take primary direct responsibility for the development of students' intellects and skills. Although few would argue that it is not the mission of higher education to assist students in the areas of intellectual and skill development, why argue that other aspects of the developing person should not intentionally be responded to as a direct and important responsibility of the institution? Is the bifurcation of a century ago that Brubacher and Rudy (1976) recognized still in evidence or in a period of revival? Is it not possible that institutions are doing students a disservice by focusing upon selected aspects to the detriment of a balanced education? Education is more than intellectual development alone, and the intellect cannot grow in healthy ways without the whole person being involved. The argument that a student's total development rests with the individual student is telling, but is it any less telling for the intellectual and skill development areas than for total development? The distinction is erroneous and at best supports the positions of those who view intellectual development as an end in itself and as being largely unrelated to the real world in which people live and seek to survive. The process of higher education cannot, and perhaps should not, seek to be all things to all people. It does have a primary responsibility to assist students in developing their intellects and the skills so necessary for survival and the enhancement of a higher quality of life. It also has a responsibility to assist students in developing as whole people and in becoming autonomous, competent, responsible, and interdependent individuals who use their intellects and skills with wisdom and integrity. It is shortsighted, indeed, to intentionally limit the mission of American higher education to intellectual development. Student affairs practitioners have recognized this fact for generations. It may be their "cross to bear," but it is essential that they seek to educate others in the campus community of these facts as well.

The primary responsibility of student affairs professionals is to assist students in their personal growth, development, and education. Typically, this is accomplished through means other than instruction in an academic discipline, although instructional methodologies are increasingly in evidence. The vehicles most commonly used to reach students include residence halls, computer programs, student centers, student activities and organizations, learning centers, counseling and career programs, work-study programs, and related environmental support services and resources. The process most commonly involved is one of challenge and response. The institution seeks to offer support and be responsive to the student's need to cope with greater levels of complexity and to master the life skills and competencies required to successfully accomplish the developmental tasks with which he or she is faced. Since human development is cumulative and continuous in nature and tends to require individuals to learn to manage increasingly complex tasks, it seems only logical that educational institutions would intentionally strive to aid students in this process. Much of education is learning how —

to learn, cope, lead, follow, solve problems, make decisions, relate to others, handle stress, and otherwise effectively function in an increasingly complex world. Are these the kinds of skills the Carnegie Commission report was referring to in its reference to intellectual and skill development? Probably not. Although these skills and competencies are essential to one's quality of life, one's effectiveness in using the intellect, and one's general level of success as a human being, they are not likely to be effectively developed by college students unless they are deliberately included as part of the experience intended to result from exposure to higher education. In other words, student affairs professionals and others in the academic community cannot leave totally to chance the learning of the essential life skills. This is not to imply that some students will not be able to learn these skills on their own or that only student affairs practitioners are responsible. It does suggest, however, that it is the responsibility of higher education to intentionally include these important developmental concerns as part of the institutional mission.

The Place of Assessment in Student Development

In many ways, assessment is the glue that holds the developmental processes together. Development by its very nature implies change, movement, and direction. Programs of intentional student development, therefore, represent deliberate attempts to facilitate the developmental process and usually seek to give it direction as well. One definition of student development, for instance, uses the mastery of increasingly complex developmental tasks and the achievement of self-direction and interdependence to give it directionality (Miller and Prince, 1976). Although there is such a thing as negative development — that is, deterioration or atavism that reflects regressions to simpler, less complex levels of functioning — such development can only be viewed as an aberration where human beings are involved. Student development, then, as represented in the application of human development principles to those involved in the college as learners, reflects growth that is purposeful, positive, and powerful.

Assessment, as a tool available to every individual as well as to every institutional organization and program, is of the essence where developmental processes are concerned. If one has direction, purpose can usually be implied. If one has purpose, goals and objectives are typically involved. If one has goals and objectives, it is then important to understand what changes are necessary to achieve them. If one knows what changes are needed, it is possible to determine what it will take to bring them about. If one knows what is yet to be accomplished, plans can be made and resources can be identified to reach them. If one has plans and access to the available resources, there is action involved. If the action results in accomplishment of the original purpose, then one has achieved some portion of a developmental task and moves on to more advanced, more complex, and more mature levels of development. And, throughout this process, assessment has been much in evidence, for it makes available the data to be analyzed and interpreted that moves the process onward to completion.

Assessment involves measurement and analysis of some kind (Lenning, 1980). As can be surmised from examining the developmental processes outlined above, there are numerous points at which data must be gathered and interpreted in order for the next step to be taken. The data gathered reflect some form of measurement, and the interpretations made are based upon analytical techniques or procedures. Although the forms may vary, the assessment processes are basically similar for most developmental processes. Assessment, when viewed from this perspective, represents a series of actions that interlock with the development process, tending to hold the whole process together and helping to make it progress smoothly from one step to the next. It is hypothesized that these assessments, or linking pins, are as applicable to cognitive development as they are to psychosocial development, although they may not be nearly so obvious.

The assessment that is initiated throughout this process may take a number of different forms, may be performed by a number of different people, and may be viewed as either a natural or a forced process, depending upon who is involved and how the process is implemented. In some instances, individual students may carry out the total process alone, while, in others, they may seek to involve others in the process.

Sometimes formal assessment techniques and instruments are called for, while, at other times, informal approaches may appear more appropriate. Basically, there is no "right" assessment procedure or approach, because each individual, group, and organization is unique and has different needs and capacities. What is important is that institutions make available qualified personnel who can help individual students, as well as student groups and organizations, gather and analyze data both to aid them in their development and to help them learn to use assessment processes and procedures on their own. Possessing expertise in the use of assessment instruments, techniques, and processes is valuable to a campus resource, but possessing expertise in how to instruct others to use them is of even greater value.

Assessment comes in many forms, and it is important that members of the campus community be knowledgeable and competent in initiating and/or instructing others in the many alternatives available. Some of the more common assessment techniques used by student affairs practitioners include career development assessment, competency/skill assessment, needs assessment, assessment of developmental task achievement, and environmental assessment. Formal assessment instruments (such as interest inventories, career search inventories, study skills tests, learning style inventories, developmental task inventories, and environmental satisfaction scales) are often useful, as are more subjective assessment approaches (such as interview techniques, self-report procedures, behavioral observations and charting, brainstorming, and values clarification). All such instruments and approaches have in common the intent of gathering measurement data and information that can be analyzed and interpreted by, for, or with students to aid in their development. Without reasonably accurate and understandable data, developmental change will at best be spasmodic and largely a result of chance factors, rather than of purposeful planning and applied action.

Not only is assessment an essential aspect of the individual student's development, it is equally useful to both organizational and staff development, both of which are so important to the profession. As professionals seek to strengthen their organizational structures and the competencies of those involved, assessment procedures and processes become increasingly important. Whether it is used for the clarification of tasks, the implementation of technology, the processing of communications, or the selection and training of personnel, assessment has great utility and must be used if the developmental programs and processes are to benefit the students who experience them. All student affairs practitioners, as well as others in the higher education community, need to carefully ascertain their purposes, goals, and objectives, as well as the strategies to achieve them. Ascertaining these important elements calls for assessment, and practitioners need to possess the essential skills and competencies required to gather measurement data and to analyze it. Developmental theory explains the processes by which development occurs and also identifies the tasks that must be achieved and the special skills that must be mastered for development to occur. If our professional goal is to create environments that are conducive to accomplishing these tasks and developing these skills, then it is necessary to find ways and means to bring such environments into existence. If our professional goal is to make people available who are qualified and competent to aid students in the developmental process and to work with them both directly and indirectly to this end, then it is necessary to identify people who are well qualified and to educate others to become competent to carry out the task. Nearly any type of development calls for assessment, and it is important that student affairs practitioners learn to use it as a normal part of their daily activity with students and programs. If a goal is worth setting, it is worth achieving, and assessment techniques are essential to accomplishing nearly any goal that can be set.

References

American Council on Education. *The Student Personnel Point of View*. American Council on Education Studies, Series 1, *1* (3). Washington, D.C.: American Council on Education, 1937.

American Council on Education. *The Student Personnel Point of View*. (Rev. ed.) American Council on Education Studies, Series, 6, *13* (13). Washington, D.C.: American Council on Education, 1949.

Brubacher, J. S., and Rudy, W. *Higher Education in Transition: A History of American Colleges and Universities, 1636–1976*. (Rev. ed.) New York: Harper & Row, 1976.

Carnegie Commission on Higher Education. *The Purposes and Performance of Higher Education in the United States*. New York: McGraw-Hill, 1973.

Chickering, A. *Education and Identity*. San Francisco: Jossey-Bass, 1969.

Chickering, A. W. *Commuting Versus Residence Students: Overcoming Educational Inequities of Living Off Campus*. San Francisco: Jossey-Bass, 1974.

Erikson, E. H. *Childhood and Society*. (2nd. ed.) New York: Norton, 1963.

Findley, J. P. "Origin and Development of the Work of the Dean of Men." *Bulletin of the Association of American Colleges*, 1939, *25*, 279–280.

Havighurst, R. J. *Human Development and Education*. New York: Longman, 1953.

Heath, D. *Growing Up in College: Liberal Education and Maturity*. San Francisco: Jossey-Bass, 1968.

Herbst, J. "The First Three American Colleges: Schools of the Reformation." *Perspectives in American History*, 1974, *8*, 7–52.

Kohlberg, L. "Stages and Sequence: The Cognitive-Developmental Approach to Socialization." In D. P. Goslin (Ed.), *Handbook of Socialization Theory and Research*. Chicago: Rand-McNally, 1969.

Lenning, O. T. "Assessment and Evaluation." In U. Delworth, G. R. Hanson, and Associates (Eds.), *Student Services: A Handbook for the Profession*. San Francisco: Jossey-Bass, 1980.

Leonard, E. A. *Origins of Personnel Services in American Higher Education*. Minneapolis: University of Minnesota Press, 1956.

Lewin, K. *Principles of Topological Psychology*. New York: McGraw-Hill, 1936.

Miller, T. K., and Prince, J. S. *The Future of Student Affairs: A Guide to Student Development for Tomorrow's Higher Education*. San Francisco: Jossey-Bass, 1976.

Moos, R. "Conceptualizations of Environment." *American Psychologist*, 1973, *28*, 652–665.

Perry, W. G., Jr. *Forms of Intellectual and Ethical Development in the College Years*. New York: Holt, Rinehart and Winston, 1970.

Piaget, J. *The Origins of Intelligence in Children*. New York: International Universities Press, 1952.

Rudolph, F. *The American College and University: A History*. New York: Random House, 1962.

Sanford, N. *Where Colleges Fail*. San Francisco: Jossey-Bass, 1967.

Wrenn, C. G. "The Development of Student Personnel Work in the United States and Some Guidelines for the Future." In M. J. Minter (Ed.), *The Student and the System*. Boulder, Colo.: Western Interstate Commission on Higher Education, 1968.

Theodore K. Miller is professor of education in the Department of Counseling and Human Development Services in the College of Education, University of Georgia. He is also director of the Center for Student Development and coordinator of the Student Personnel in Higher Education Preparation Program.

Social-cognitive development is not completed
during the undergraduate college years; therefore,
when college students are faced with developmental tasks
that require complex decision making, they end up
in a developmental double bind.

Human Development and the College Campus: Sequences and Tasks

Karen Strohm Kitchener

Despite the fact that student development has been touted as a goal, if not the most important goal for student services, it has not always been clear what constitutes development, what aspects of the person are developing, or what developmental aspects might be important or relevant to student service professionals. At the same time, it is clear to those who work with college students that important changes are taking place in how they think about themselves, how they relate to peers, how they think through intellectual problems, how they see themselves in relation to work, and so forth. Numerous authors (Astin, 1977; Chickering, 1969; Davis, 1977; Heath, 1968; Heath, 1964) have spent years investigating and conceptualizing the nature of these changes. Despite their work, however, confusion continues about the nature of development.

The field of development has remained in disorder for at least three reasons. First, people writing on development have diverse roots. They represent different psychological and sometimes sociological tra-

The author wishes to thank James R. Davis, Kurt W. Fischer, and Patricia M. King for reading and commenting on an earlier version of this chapter.

G. R. Hanson (Ed.). *Measuring Student Development.* New Directions for Student Services, no. 20. San Francisco: Jossey-Bass, December 1982.

ditions. In many ways, the status of developmental psychology is no different from the status of counseling or clinical psychology. Writers conceptualize development out of the behavioral, cognitive-developmental, differential, humanistic, and psychodynamic traditions. Each assumes a different model of the nature of people and conceptualizes change in a unique way.

Secondly, the field of college student development has been in particular disarray because theory and research on college students have often evolved outside of the general developmental tradition. As a consequence, the literature on college students and more general developmental theory have seldom been integrated or cross-referenced. Up until ten years ago, developmental psychologists, whose roots were in child psychology, focused their attention on infancy, childhood, and early adolescence. People investigating college student development often had their roots in higher education (Astin, 1977; Chickering, 1969; Davis, 1977; Heath, 1968). As a consequence, two separate traditions arose.

The third reason for confusion is really a consequence of the other two. In some areas there is a great deal of information about development but it is contradictory or nonintegrated. In other areas there is too little information. For example, Chickering (1969), Erikson (1963, 1968), Heath (1968), Heath (1964), Loevinger (1976), and Perry (1970) have all written on aspects of the self, identity, and ego. It is not always apparent, however, how these models complement each other or to what extent they are contradictory. By contrast, other areas of development have been virtually ignored. For example, Drum (1980) hypothesizes seven dimensions of student development. These include cognitive structure, aesthetic development, identity formation, physical self, moral reasoning, interpersonal relationships, and social perspective. While his model is both useful and interesting, three of the dimensions (aesthetic development, physical self, and social perspective) are only tangentially discussed by most theorists, if mentioned at all. No standard assessment instruments are available to measure these aspects of development and no systematic research has been done that would confirm or disprove their existence. This is true despite the fact that there is some face validity to assuming that development may or ought to occur in these areas.

To impose some order on the confusion, this chapter will begin with a general discussion of the nature of development and the influences on it. Secondly, it will place college student development in the broader context of lifespan development in order to compare what it is to be a highly developed college student with what it is to be a highly developed adult. Third, it will focus on describing social-cognitive developmental sequences and normative age-related tasks. A discussion of developmental sequences will provide a framework for understanding similarities and differences in the cognitive complexity of students across different domains. The developmental task model will identify different developmental needs for traditional-aged and older college students. These are complementary models of development. The first model provides a map of major changes in reasoning style. The second outlines age-related changes in skills, attitudes, and interests.

In the discussion of these models, the diverse threads from developmental psychology and college student development have been integrated. For discussions of particular theorists' models, the reader may consult the original sources listed in the references.

The Nature of Development

Definitions of Development. Most writers would agree that development involves age-related changes, both quantitative and qualitative, in the human organism (Loevinger, 1976; Shaie and Geiwitz, 1982; Whitbourne and Weinstock, 1979; Wohlwill, 1973), although some (Baltes, Reese, and Lipsitt, 1980) would even omit the reference to age. Development can be thought of as potentially encompassing changes in behavior, physical abilities, cognitive structure, intellectual abilities, social interactions and roles, and so forth. In other words, almost any aspect of the organism that changes with the passage of time and life experiences can be thought of as developing. These changes can occur throughout the lifespan. They may take place as a consequence of physical maturation or deterioration, influences of the environment, or an interaction between the current status of the organism and the environment.

The use of the term *change* is a deliberate one, for it does not imply directionality. Some developmental psychologists (Baltes, Reese, and Lipsitt, 1980; Neugarten, 1968) argue that they are interested in patterns of change in abilities, structures, and behavior. These changes may include deterioration, as well as extension or progression.

The ambivalence about specifying the direction of change associated with the term *development* arose because little was known about the changes that transpired in the adult years, so individuals writing on development were hesitant to speculate about the direction of change. In fact, until recently, cross-sectional data on intellectual abilities was interpreted to mean that intelligence increased until the mid-twenties and then declined (Schaie and Geiwitz, 1982).

Despite the general ambivalence about specifying the direction of change, the focus of this chapter will be on aspects of development for which there is growth potential. This is both the most common understanding of the term *development* and the kind of change student affairs professionals assume when they talk about promoting development. Promoting development implies that there is room to enhance some aspect of the person.

Lifespan Development. The belief that an individual's development at any particular point in time needs to be understood in terms of the sequence of events and processes that begin at birth and continue to death is not a new one (Baltes, Reese, and Lipsitt, 1980). There has, however, been an explosion of research and speculation in this area in the last decade that has begun to provide us with more comprehensive models of development (Fischer, 1980; Kohlberg, 1976; Levinson, 1978; Sheehy, 1976) and has popularized the idea that life does not end at age eighteen.

The concept of lifespan development is important for a comprehensive picture of student development for two reasons. First, not all college students are between the ages of eighteen and twenty-one. Women are returning to school in their thirties. Men are making career changes in their forties, and both are seeking education in new areas after retirement. In some cases, gifted high school students are attending college classes for advanced learning opportunities. If educators in universities and colleges are really interested in the full range of students, they must understand the developmental differences and similarities between young adults and older ones.

Secondly, a life span perspective provides a more realistic viewpoint within which to understand college students. Normally, an individual's college career spans only four to five years; a relatively short period of time in the life of most people. Many attend for shorter periods and only a few attend for longer. Some models of college student development have been overly optimistic about how much development can be expected to occur in the four years traditional undergraduates attend college.

Social-Cognitive Development

Social-cognitive development encompasses what others have referred to as the cognitive-developmental (Parker, Widick, and Knefelkamp, 1978); organismic (Lerner, 1976); hierarchical, classical (Emmerich, 1968), and structural-adaptive theories (Drum, 1980). The best known proponent of this model is Piaget (1970) although the work of Harvey, Hunt, and Schroder (1961), Kohlberg (1976), Loevinger (1976), and Perry (1970) would fall under this rubric.

The basic concern of social-cognitive developmental theorists is with orderly changes in reasoning patterns. Reasoning patterns act as filters through which an individual ascribes meaning to an event, issue, or problem. In other words, learning, understanding, and problem solving are affected by the nature of the reasoning pattern a person holds. Development occurs when an event, idea, or action cannot be assimilated or absorbed without distorting either the reasoning pattern or the stimulus. A new stimulus or event forces a reorganization of the current thought pattern. Through this process more complex and adequate ways of reasoning are formed.

What is more, development proceeds sequentially through several stages, levels, or positions. Each level represents a qualitatively different form of thinking or approaching and conceptualizing a problem. The interpretation individuals give to an event, issue, or problem will vary, therefore, with their developmental level. Most theorists argue that higher points in a developmental sequence allow more adequate interpretations of an event and provide better problem-solving strategies because they require less distortion of an event or idea and provide for more complex processing.

While Piaget (1970) argued that the development of logical thinking could account for the increased complexity of reasoning in all areas, more recently others (Fischer, 1980; Kitchener and Kitchener, 1981; Kohlberg, 1976; Loevinger, 1976) have suggested that concepts of knowledge, self, morality and relationships follow their own developmental sequences. The developmental sequence in each area is unique because of differences in content; however, the general principles underlying development across content areas are similar. In this respect social concepts and reasoning (for example, about relationships, self, morality) appear to develop in the same way (for example, sequentially) as do concepts in the intellectual domain (such as knowledge or logic.)

The highest point in each sequence identifies the end goal of development. The sequence itself specifies the steps that lead to the goal. It should not be assumed, however, that all people develop to the highest level in all areas. Some environments will lack sufficient stimulation to facilitate development. For this reason, a stage or level may not be perfectly or even well predicted by age. This is especially true after adolescence, as environmental influences become more diverse and less predictable.

While there is considerable agreement within the social-cognitive developmental school that reasoning becomes more complex, there has been disagreement about when development ceases, how much synchrony to expect across different developmental sequences, and whether developmental change is abrupt or gradual. Although there are descriptive and conceptual similarities between some models (for example, Loevinger's model (1976) contains an aspect she calls character development that appear to be descriptively similar to Kohlberg's (1976) stages of moral development), there has been no unifying theory that would allow one to decide which model is more accurate or to predict new developmental sequences (such as a sequence of increasingly complex assumptions about sex roles).

Part of the problem has been that Piaget, who formulated the basis for a cognitive-developmental model (Piaget, 1970), assumed that structural development ceased in adolescence with the emergence of hypothetico-deductive thinking. Further change, he argued, was a consequence of assuming adult roles that led the individual away from the self-centeredness of adolescence into the reality-based thinking of mature adulthood (Inhelder and Piaget, 1958). While others (Arlin, 1975; Fischer, 1980; Riegal, 1979) have challenged this assumption, no other comprehensive model of social-cognitive development has been available until recently.

Fischer's Model of Social-Cognitive Development. Fischer (1980) has proposed a model of social-cognitive development that spans the period from infancy to the middle adult years and may be generalized to reach even further into adulthood. The model is a valuable framework for understanding college student development because it provides a method for (1) assessing and comparing current development models, (2) identifying the general nature of change, (3) predicting the amount of consistency that should be expected across areas, and (4) predicting new developmental sequences.

Fischer (1980) uses simple set theory to describe the emergence of ten levels of intellectual functioning. Changes in level, he suggests, may be tied to biological changes in brain functioning (Fischer, Hand, and Russell, forthcoming). The ten levels are organized into three tiers: the sensorimotor, the representational, and the abstract. Since the first three levels form the sensorimotor tier and refer only to development in infancy, they will not be discussed here. Fischer suggests that in childhood the representational tier, which is composed of four levels, develops. The fourth level of representational skills becomes the first level of the abstract tier, which also develops through four levels (Table 1).

The first level of the representational tier begins with a single, simple concept or skill that designates a concrete characteristic of objects, events, or people. Drawing from the area of social roles, an individual might have the single concept of woman as his or her particular mother. Similarly, in the area of moral reasoning, the single concept may be that morality (goodness or badness) is determined by whether one gets punished or not. At the second level of the representational tier, an individual can relate two simple, concrete concepts or sets. At level three, the individual can break each of the simple concrete concepts down into its subparts and, therefore, understand each more completely.

The fourth level of the representational tier, called a system of systems, allows individuals to construct two complex representational sets into an interrelated system. This fourth representational level forms the first level of the abstract tier and marks the emergence of simple abstractions. The second abstract level parallels the second representational level and so on. Specifically, at the second abstract level, simple abstractions can be related to each other. Similarly, at the third abstract level, the individual forms abstract systems in which two or more abstract ideas can be broken into their subparts and their subparts related to each other. The fourth and highest level of the abstract tier, a system of abstract systems, allows two abstract systems to be related to each other. Conceivably, this system of abstract systems could form the basis for an even higher, as yet unidentified, developmental tier.

Fischer's model gives form to the observations of Loevinger (1976), Harvey, Hunt and Schroder (1961), Kitchener and King (1981), Kohlberg (1976), and Perry (1970) that initial concepts are singular, absolute, and concrete. Initially, the number of concepts, their differentiation, and complexity increases. Simple abstractions emerge as two or more of these complex, concrete concepts combine to form a new type of concept. Last, the ability to interrelate abstract concepts allows for the emergence of truly mature thinking about moral issues, the self, knowledge, and so forth.

A second important aspect of Fischer's model is its generalizability. He suggests that it should be applicable to cognitive structures or skills of any kind (for example, interpersonal, artistic, intellectual, athletic). We should be able to define a developmental sequence for each by applying the basic model of tiers and levels within tiers. He goes on to suggest, however, that unless there is an overlap between the network of skills or concepts on one domain (for example, concepts of morality) and another (for example, relationships concepts), development in one area will not necessarily lead to further development in another area.

Table 1. Levels of Social-Cognitive Development

Fischer's Model[a]	Concepts of Knowledge[b]	Concepts of Morality[c]	Concepts of Relationship[d]	Concepts of Self[e]
Representational Level I: Single, Concrete Concepts. Diagramed: •	Single category for knowing: to know means to observe directly without evaluation.	Singular category for good and bad. Bad gets punished, good does not.	Single relationship category: People do what I want them to or they do not.	Single category for understanding self: Self is physical body.
Representational Level II: Can relate two simple concrete concepts. Diagramed: •—•	Two categories of knowing: People can be right about what they know or wrong.	Two category morality: for me good is what I want. For you good is what you want. Bad is the opposite.	Two category relationship concepts: Relationships are good or bad depending on events in which we participate.	Two category self concepts: Self is body or mind, or likes or dislikes.
Representational Level III: Several concrete concepts can be broken into subparts and related. Diagramed: ▢	People can be right about what they know or wrong or knowledge may be incomplete or unavailable. It may differ for different areas.	Good is being considerate, nice, and kind. Bad is opposite. This is true for self and other.	Relationships can be good and bad depending on how we act with each other.	Self is many concrete aspects: i.e., what is inside and what is outside and what I like and what I dislike.
Representational Level IV = Abstract Level I. Can relate two complex representational sets into abstract concept. Diagramed: ▣	The fact that knowledge is unknown in several instances leads to initial understanding of knowledge as an abstraction. It is seen as uncertain.	Law understood abstractly as organizing good and bad for people in general.	Group understood as nucleus for relationships. Relations are regulated via social convention.	Initial abstract concepts of self and identity: Human being consists of body and mind, what I like and what I dislike. I am human being.

Abstract Level II: Can relate two or more abstract concepts. Diagramed:	There is uncertainty in science and history and philosophy, etc. What we know is subject to interpretation. Seen as relative within a context.	Laws are different for different cultures. Good and bad interpreted in different ways. Morality is relative to time and place.	Group becomes differentiated into individuals within the group. Relationships are different with each.	Self is many abstractions: liberal and conservative, religious and agnostic, good and bad.
Abstract Level III: Abstract concepts further differentiated and related. Diagramed:	Although knowledge is uncertain and subject to interpretation, it is possible to abstract some conclusions across domains. Knowledge is outcomes of these.	While laws and good and bad are interpreted different ways at different times and places, the well being of people is a common consideration.	While relationships may differ with different people and at different times, good relationships have common characteristics, i.e., solid.	Although self is many things at different times and places, self has common core.
Abstract Level IV: System of abstractions. Higher order conceptual relationships. Diagramed:	Knowing probabilistically via inquiry unifies concepts of knowledge.	Principles, i.e., the value of human life, autonomy, doing good unify diverse concepts of morality.	Autonomous interdependence unifies concepts of individuality and commitment.	Integrated, autonomous self. Self as unique abstract different abstract concepts of self.

a. Fischer (1980). Diagram generalized from Fischer, 1980, p. 490.
b. Based on Broughton (1978), Kitchener and King (1981), Perry (1970).
c. Based on Loevinger (1976), Cooney and Selman (1978), Perry (1970).
d. Based on Kohlberg (1976), Fischer and Lazerson (1981).
e. Based on Broughton (1978), Erikson (1968), Loevinger (1976).

This hypothesis gives recognition to apparent developmental discrepancies. Loevinger (1976), for example, points to individuals who are highly skilled intellectually but whose interpersonal relationships are extremely limited. Similarly, Douglas Heath (1968) has observed that, while the pattern of maturing is similar across domains, the rate of maturing college students differs in different areas. Fischer (1980), in fact, suggests that the developmental discrepancies may be more pronounced at the abstract tier than in the earlier tiers because environmental influences are more variable at higher levels.

Fischer also argues that between levels there may be a great deal of individual variability in how progression from one level to the next occurs. This suggests that we may need to attend to quantitative differences in development as well as qualitative ones.

A third interesting aspect of Fischer's model is his claim that there is an upper limit of complexity that an individual can control at any particular time. This upper limit or optimal level shifts upward with age. In other words, the person's optimal level is a measure of his or her highest capacity for complexity. Actual development in a particular domain may not reach optimal level because of the lack of opportunity to construct the more complex functions. This concept is particularly important in understanding what may be a limit on development in traditionally aged undergraduates, since Fischer, Hand, and Russell (forthcoming) suggest that the optimal level for the highest abstractions may not be reached until age twenty-five.

The fourth aspect of Fischer's model that is relevant to understanding college students is his discussion of the relationship between a measurement task and level. Fischer argues that individuals will score at higher social-cognitive developmental levels on simpler tasks than on more complex ones. For example, if the task involves the application of a skill or concept to a real life situation, it is more likely that an individual will reason at a lower level than if the task is a laboratory example of a simple case.

One implication of this argument is that, in diagnosing an individual's developmental level, one must be aware of the measure used to assess it. A complete developmental picture or profile depends on the use of a variety of assessment techniques even in a single area (Rest, 1979). On the other hand, if we are interested in how individuals reason on complex, real world tasks, then it will be important to use an appropriate assessment format and not assume that the age range of results generated on simple examples generalizes to the real world. (See Mines' chapter in this volume for a further discussion of this point).

Developmental Sequences. Hypothetically, developmental sequences that move from simple, concrete concepts to abstract concepts to high level integrated, reflective concepts could be constructed in all of the areas in which students might be ideally developing. For purposes of illustration, Table 1 spells out in detail four developmental sequences as they might be mapped on Fischer's (1980) general model. Table 1 is based on an integration of the work of several theorists. The four areas—knowledge, morality, self, and relationships—were chosen for elaboration because they have been consistently identified by student development theorists as important and as paths along which most college students develop. A fifth sequence will be discussed in the narrative because of its critical role in intellectual development.

Intellectual Development. The intellectual domain may be broken into two aspects: logical reasoning and concepts of knowledge. While these two aspects may interact in solving any particular problem, developmentally they appear to be separate threads (Kitchener and Kitchener, 1981).

From the Concrete to the Hypothetical to the Hypothetico-Deductive. The ability to use inductive and deductive logic to reason about hypotheses in science classes, hypothetical situations in international relations, or the idealized "good" in an ethics class are skills college professors often assume students have. However, recent research (Neimark, 1975) suggests this may not be the case.

Most investigations of the development of logical reasoning come out of the Inhelder and Piaget (1958) work on formal operations. While Inhelder and Piaget suggest only one major shift in conceptual patterns between childhood and adolescence—that it, from concrete to formal operational—more recent work (Neimark, 1975, 1979) suggests that neither period is as unitary as Piaget thought them to be.

Between childhood and late adolescence, there seems to be a shift from the ability to think about concrete data-based instances to the ability to think about hypothetical situations. Later, the ability to think hypothetically becomes formalized in an interrelated system of inductive and deductive logic. This enables the individual to move from a concrete issue by issue, case by case consideration of an idea to the kind of theoretical and speculative thinking necessary for scientific inquiry. The less mature thinker can reason within and about a single proposition. The more mature thinker can reason between propositions in a deductively correct way and develop hypothetical inferences from them. Later, inductive and deductive reasoning are combined in a way that allows the individual to form a hypothesis, deduce the observations from that hypothesis that can be used to test it, and understand the relationship between data and falsification or confirmation of the hypothesis.

The data in this area is difficult to evaluate because investigators have not consistently used the same tasks or tasks of the same level of difficulty. However, while Piaget suggested that formal operations developed in early adolescence, many (Neimark, 1975; King, 1977) have found that college and university students cannot pass some or many formal operations tasks. Tomlinson-Keasey (1972) similarly found that only a little over 50 percent of her middle-aged women subjects scored as formal operational. In her reviews of formal operational research, Neimark (1975, 1979) concluded that not all adults, even educated ones in technologically advanced societies, attain formal operations when assessed for such competencies on Piagetian tasks. Findings such as these led Piaget (1972) to conclude that adults may be capable of abstract logical thinking but only on problems about which they have experience, interest, and expertise.

What does this mean for individuals working with college students? First and foremost, even when college students are adults, they may have difficulty using correct deductive and inductive logical reasoning in some problem areas. Therefore, students may have difficulty on academic or applied tasks that require logical application of content. Note, for example, the number of students who complain about the difficulty of introductory psychology tests that require not only knowledge of content but the ability to draw logical conclusions. Faculty may need help in understanding the logical limitations of their students' reasoning, and students may need help in developing logical conclusions.

From Absolutes to Uncertainty to Probabilities. Although seeing logical connections may be one important aspect of thinking through a problem, it is not the only aspect of problem solving. Two individuals may reason in logically impeccable ways, yet, because they begin with different assumptions about knowledge itself, the conclusions they reach may differ. Take the issue of whether chemical additives to food are dangerous, for example. If one individual assumes that there is an absolutely correct answer for the issue, he or she will seek sources of information (authorities, experts, books) that will tell him or her the correct answer. If, by contrast, the other individual assumes knowledge is ultimately uncertain, he or she may determine that no conclusion is more accurate than any other.

According to the work of Broughton (1978), Kitchener and King (1981), and Perry (1970), concepts of knowledge evolve from the concrete assumption that knowledge is absolute, knowable, and known by someone (usually an authority) to the abstract assumption that knowledge is uncertain. Individuals conclude that, without authorities to justify beliefs, there is no reasonable way to decide between alternative viewpoints about an issue. As a consequence, students frequently claim that "everybody has the right to their own opinion" (Perry, 1970). In other words, individuals are skeptical about ever knowing anything by means of reason.

The highest point on this sequence is a form of rationalism, probabilism, or reflective judgment. Individuals are able to integrate several abstract systems into a new perspective that is uniquely their own. While they understand that knowing absolutely is impossible because human beings filter reality through their own perspectives, they do not reject the power of reason to form better or even best solutions for problems. Through the ongoing process of inquiry, it is possible to build closer and closer approximations to the truth. Individuals claim that points of view are "measured judgments which are probably true or more or less in keeping with what the facts seem to be" (Kitchener and King, 1981, p. 100).

Where do college students lie on this continuum? First, all the studies that have been completed in this area have used complex tasks to assess development. Students have been asked to reason about real world issues (Broughton, 1978; Kitchener and King, 1981; Perry, 1970). Basing their findings on these complex tasks, investigators have consistently concluded that older, more educated subjects use more complex and differentiated concepts of knowledge. (See King, 1978; King and others, forthcoming; or Schmidt and Davison, 1981, for reviews of these data.) However, with the exception of Perry's (1970) original study, no investigators have found undergraduates who consistently use probabilistic or reflective concepts of knowledge nor has this been the case among first-year graduate students (Brabeck, 1980).

In descriptive terms, most entering college students have given up the assumption that absolute knowledge exists in all areas. In general, they use a form of reasoning similar to the third representational level on Table 1. They admit that uncertainty is real in some areas, although they may maintain that absolutes still exist (for example, in science or religion). On the average, seniors score only one-half to one full level higher (the first abstract level on Table 1) than do entering freshmen. In general, they believe that uncertainty is the rule and are skeptical about the potential of reason to solve problems. Shoff (1979) and Strange and King (1977) find that older men and women returning to school do not score significantly higher than traditionally aged college students. Doctoral level graduate students (King and others, forthcoming; Mines, 1980) have been found to use the highest reasoning type even on complex tasks; however, not even all doctoral level graduate students consistently use this form of reasoning.

A few individuals (Mason, 1978, Stephenson, and Hunt, 1977; Widick, Knefelkamp, and Parker, 1975) have investigated the effects of interventions designed to promote more complex thinking about concepts of knowledge. Using undergraduate or master's level college students, they found positive pre-post differences after semester long developmentally designed courses. Gains were, however, small. Undergraduates were not scored as using the most complex concepts of knowledge even after the interventions.

What does this mean for student affairs professionals? First, it suggests that, when students reason about complex tasks, they will probably be skeptical about the potential of reason to solve problems. Upon entering college, some will still cling to the belief that absolute knowledge exists in some areas and they will look for authorities who have that knowledge. These authorities may be their counselors, residence hall directors, teachers, advisers, or faculty members. They may later express disillusionment with these same people for not knowing the absolute truth. The emotional and intellectual turmoil this realization causes students should not be underestimated. Here, Sanford's (1966) observation that support is as critical for development as is challenge is most insightful. Students often feel confused about how judgments may be made when absolutes disappear. They spend much of the remainder of their undergraduate years trying to understand how anything can be known under such circumstances.

Secondly, reasoning about real world issues does not advance as high or as fast as most educators would like and many assume (Drum, 1980). Undergraduates do not reason probabilistically. At the same time, many college professors and programs assume students are capable of using such a reasoning style. As a consequence of the accumulating research in this area, educators may need to reassess their goals for undergraduate students.

From Punishment to Legalistic to Principled. Individuals writing about college student development have consistently emphasized changes in the nature of moral values during the college years (Chickering, 1969; Heath, 1968; Perry, 1970). Astin (1977) and Chickering (1969), for example, report increases in altruism and a general decline in a conservative orientation. Up until fifteen years ago, however, most research focused on changes in the content of values rather than on the form of reasoning individuals exhibit when faced with a moral problem.

Based on a social-cognitive developmental model, seven levels of development in moral reasoning can be mapped (Table 1). At each level, the conceptual tools available for moral decision making become more complete because they rest on increasingly complex concepts of fairness and justice.

Initially, moral reasoning is simple, concrete, and based on external consequences. Something is bad if I get caught and punished. It is good if I do not get punished. This form of moral reasoning is found typically among young children.

The first abstract level in this sequence allows the individual to understand that law coordinates the actions of many individuals and, therefore, forms a more ultimate test of the "goodness" or "badness" of an action. The ultimate test of the morality of an action becomes its legal status — that is, whether it coincides with the law. At the second abstract level, the belief that law coordinates the actions of individuals is seen through a relativistic perspective — that is, law is understood as being different for different cultures and different historical periods. Whether an action is judged to be moral or immoral depends on the context. Something can be right for one person, in a particular time and place, but wrong for someone else, at a different time or place (Gilligan and Murphy, 1979). Ultimately, at abstract level four, the individual reintegrates and coordinates his or her understanding of fairness and moral consequences, arguing that general moral principles exist that are more basic than and even supercede cultural differences. At this level, the individual may have a concern for the welfare of all persons and for the ultimate goodness of life itself. These general principles, therefore, become the most ultimate test of the morality of an action.

Kohlberg's (1976) theory of moral judgment has provided the framework for much of the research on the development of moral concepts during the past two decades. It is difficult, however, to draw conclusions about the moral judgment of college students from the studies based on his moral development theory. The difficulty stems from his use of an interview to assess level of moral reasoning. There have been numerous changes in his scoring system (Colby, 1978) during the past twenty years, which means that data scored with an early scoring scheme are not comparable with data scored on the current system. Kohlberg (1978) has claimed, however, that very few adults use principled moral reasoning when their reasoning is assessed with his interview procedure.

Rest (1979, 1981) has developed the most comprehensive body of data on moral reasoning. His data are based on an objective measure of moral judgment that requires individuals to recognize and appreciate different forms of moral thinking when they see it. He has found a consistent relationship between higher levels of moral reasoning and educational level (1981). In fact, the correlation between moral judgment scores and education has been consistently higher than the correlation between moral reasoning and age. Moral reasoning scores plateau after individuals leave formal educational settings. This finding suggests that it would be inaccurate to expect adults who return to school to use a higher level of moral reasoning than the traditionally aged college student. Rest (1981) has also found that students who do not live at home show larger increases in moral judgment scores than do those who remain at home while attending college.

Several studies have looked at the effects of short-term (two to six months) interventions on moral judgment development. Of the eight studies that included students in higher education, several reported significant pre-post gains in moral judgment score (Lawrence, 1980). These gains were, however, small, and in no case did an intervention lead students to consistently use principled reasoning. Rest (1979) concludes that we should expect changes in moral judgment to occur slowly because they involve basic reorganizations in thinking patterns. These patterns probably change over the course of many educational experiences that encourage individuals to reformulate their basic perspective about society and morality.

There are two aspects of this work on the development of moral reasoning that are significant for student affairs professionals. First, while students may recognize moral principles as important and valuable to moral judgment, they will probably be unable to use such principles in reasoning about real world problems. In their own reasoning, they will probably fall back on legal or social codes as the basis for moral decisions. Others may declare that values are relative to time and place and use this as a license to pursue an "anything goes" form of morality. If Rest's (1981) data is correct, both groups of students will move to a more principled and complex form of moral reasoning with increased education.

Second, student affairs professionals should note that short term interventions have limited value in promoting moral judgment. We should not expect students to use the most complex and integrated form of moral reasoning after such interventions.

From Self as the Concrete Body to an Initial Identity to Autonomy. Many have noted that college students' self-concepts undergo radical revision (Chickering, 1969; Erikson, 1968; Marcia, 1980). Only recently have writers begun, however, to approach this issue from a cognitive-developmental perspective (Broughton, 1978; Cooney and Selman, 1978; Fischer and Lazerson, 1981; Loevinger, 1976).

As in other social-cognitive domains, the general pattern of change moves from concrete and simple to abstract to integrated and reflective (Table 1). Taking this perspective, it is not accurate to think of an individual as having or developing a single, unchanging identity. Rather, self-concepts or identity shift gradually and become more complex over a period of time (Marcia, 1980). In early childhood, concepts of self are simple and concrete. Children view themselves through single categories — that is, their physical bodies. With age and experience, the number of categories available for understanding themselves increases. They may see themselves as what is inside (their mind) or outside (their physical appearance). Later, they may see themselves as potentially both what is inside and outside at the same time, without being able to integrate both aspects into the abstract concept of a human being who consists of both parts.

Cooney and Selman (1978) and Broughton (1978) suggest that this notion of the self first appears in individuals at about age twelve. They also note, however, that there are adults who do not move beyond this point developmentally. In fact, it is not infrequent to hear college students comment on the difference between the "real me" that is inside and their physical self, which is only their appearance. It may be that, developmentally, when dealing with their own identity in the real world, some students remain confused about how to fully integrate both aspects into a single concept of self.

At the first abstract level, individuals can think of themselves with simple abstractions (for example, as a human being, as a liberal, as religious). These abstractions form the basis for an initial abstract identity. However, at this level, two abstract aspects of themselves cannot be related. Later, the individual can compare abstract concepts but he or she still appears contradictory — that is, may see himself or herself as liberal in some cases and conservative in others (Fischer and Lazerson, 1981). The inability to coordinate apparently contradictory aspects of an abstract identity may lead to what Erikson has called identity diffusion. Marcia (1980) reports that this is a problem for significant numbers of college students.

At abstract level four, individuals can coordinate the many abstract concepts of themselves into a single integrated system. They can see themselves as autonomous (that is, with an identity independent of a particular time, place, or event). In addition, their identity integrates apparent contradictions into a unique whole. Broughton suggests that the concept of self as autonomous does not initially emerge until age twenty-five plus.

Although it is unlikely that college students will hold single category concepts of themselves, it is possible that some will enter college with relatively concrete and nonintegrated self-concepts. At best they will see themselves as contradictory and their identity will be unstable. For student affairs professionals, this may mean that students will understand themselves as different at different times and places and, therefore, may act in contradictory ways. It may also mean that college provides an important atmosphere in which students try on several identities before integrating these identities into a whole. Last, it may mean that many students are confused about who they are and this confusion may lead to considerable turmoil.

Information about the effectiveness of interventions designed specifically to promote development along this dimension can only be inferred indirectly from studies using Loevinger and Wessler's (Loevinger and Wessler, 1970) test of ego development. The findings are similar to those in the areas of moral and intellectual development. While some studies have found significant pre–post differences (Loevinger, 1979), these differences have not been large. Subjects have not held autonomous concepts of themselves by the end of the interventions.

From Unilateral to Conformist to Autonomous Interdependence. As with the development of self-concepts, the sequence of relationship concepts proposed here is based on the work of several theorists (Cooney and Selman, 1978; Heath, 1968; Loevinger, 1976; Perry, 1970). It reflects the general observation that with age and maturity, relationships are understood more complexly and are less tied to the outcome of specific interactions.

More specifically, in childhood, relationships are understood by means of a simple, singular concrete category. In a sense, relationships are not relationships, for they are understood unilaterally (for example, you either do what I want you to do or you do not). Loevinger (1976) notes the exploitative and dependent character of such interactions. The concept of relationships as involving reciprocal actions does not evolve until later and is probably characteristic of representational level III (Table 1).

The concept of the group as providing social norms or conventions that regulate interpersonal relationships may emerge at the first abstract level. Here, particular relationships can be understood as one example or subset of relationships in general. Loevinger (1976) has commented on the conformist quality of relationships conceptualized in this way. Data derived from Loevinger's work (1979) suggest that this concept of relationships is common by adolescence.

Moving beyond the conception of relationships conforming to a social norm, individuals begin to differentiate people with the group and to understand that different reciprocal relationships are appropriate with each. Assuming this concept of relationships is typified by Loevinger's (1976) conscientious-conformist (I-3/4) and conscientious (I-4) stages; studies of college students and adults (Hauser, 1976; Kitchener and others, 1982; Loevinger, 1979) suggest that these assumptions about relationships are most common. Perhaps environmental circumstances that stimulate more complex concepts of interpersonal relationships are rare, and many people do not experience the conditions necessary to promote further growth. It is also possible that Loevinger's test is not sensitive to higher-level changes.

Loevinger (1976) and others (Cooney and Selman, 1978; Heath, 1968; Perry, 1970) have postulated that there is potential, however, for a more abstract and differentiated concept of relationships. They suggest that the highest level is characterized by a respect for individuality and commitment or autonomous interdependence. Individuals may experience good and bad times together, but the relationship is greater than the sum total of these events. Similarly, the relationship exists concurrently with deep valuing of individual differences. It is probably unlikely that relationship concepts such as these develop until the adult years — that is, until twenty-five years and older.

Conclusions

Before moving to discussion of developmental tasks, it may be useful to summarize some general conclusions about social-cognitive sequences.

While the specific content of a sequence differs in different areas, development is generally from simple, concrete categories to simple abstract categories to highly differentiated, integrated and reflective categories. Although only five such sequences have been discussed, others that are of importance for college populations could be identified. For example, it is probably the case that concepts of sex roles progress through similar levels of conceptual complexity.

Social-cognitive developmental sequences measure epochal development. Under normal conditions, four or more years may lapse between developmental levels and, in fact, biological changes in the brain functioning may place some limits on how fast development may occur (Fischer, Hand, and Russell, forthcoming). Fine-grained development is difficult to capture with such models.

On the other hand, each level in a sequence represents a qualitatively distinct thought pattern that influences understanding and problem solving in a particular domain. At each higher level, reasoning becomes more adequate, complex, and differentiated.

Development along these sequences does occur during the undergraduate years. As measured by real-life tasks, this development may involve some residual aspects of representation level III. In general, however, movement is from abstract level I to abstract level II. The beginning of abstract level III may be observed in some simple tasks. It is probably best to think of the highest point in these developmental sequences as occurring with individuals over the age of twenty-five.

While some short-term interventions, designed to produce development, have shown pre–post differences, these differences are small. Development appears to be a slow process that may involve periods of advancement and then consolidation. Several experiences within the same domain may be necessary before thought patterns are reorganized. The cumulative effect of higher education in stimulating moral and intellectual development appears particularly important.

Developmental Tasks

According to developmental task theorists (Havighurst, 1972; Erikson, 1963; Levinson, 1978; Sheehy, 1976), life is divided into periods that are marked by a concern with and a need to accomplish certain tasks. These tasks, which involve developing new attitudes, roles, and skills, become critical because of the convergence of social expectations and physiological maturation. For example, in the United States, after a youth graduates from high school, it is socially expected that he or she will leave home and establish a career. These two expectations force the youth into considering and reconsidering who he or she is in relationship to the family and to the world at large. As a consequence, the youth would need to establish a work identity and instrumental independence (Chickering, 1969). The social forces on a woman in her thirties whose children have all entered school would be different from the forces at work on a youth of eighteen, and, therefore, the developmental tasks would differ.

The assumption of many theorists in this area has been that age-appropriate skills must be learned if the individual is going to move successfully into the next life period. The problem with this perspective, however, is that many individuals whose lives appear out of sequence — that is, who do not develop skills or take on roles at the appropriate times — often establish effective adult lifestyles. This is especially true for many of the tasks associated with adolescents and adults. For example, establishing a marital relationship and having children have been identified as developmental tasks of young adulthood (Havighurst, 1972), yet in-

creasing numbers of individuals are choosing to remain unmarried and/
or are having children in their mid-thirties.

In contrast to this strict developmental task approach, Baltes,
Reese, and Lipsitt (1980) have pointed to three kinds of influences on individual development. Developmental tasks that are a consequence of
these three kinds of influences are still important, although the exact nature of these tasks, their order, and their importance is more variable
than has been thought in the past.

The Baltes, Reese, and Lipsitt Model

Normative Age-Graded Influences. Certain events happen at
about the same time for most people because of age-related similarities
in biological clocks and the demands of our social institutions. Baltes,
Reese, and Lipsitt (1980) call these normative age-graded influences.
They are identical with the influences developmental task theorists
thought were primarily responsible for the age-related need to accomplish certain tasks. Sexual maturity, leaving home, and the entrance of
the last child into school are all examples. These influences lead to the
need to develop specific skills or to take on new roles and attitudes — for
example, to cope with children leaving home or identify an initial career
choice.

Normative History-Graded Influences. A second set of influences
that carries demands for the cultivation of new skills has been called normative, history-graded, or generational. They are defined as "biological
and environmental determinants associated with historical time"
(Baltes, Reese, and Lipsitt, 1980, p. 75). They are normative and historical because they occur to most members of society who live through a
particular historical period but not to members of a different generation
who did not experience the historical event. Examples of such events
might be the Vietnam war, the Depression, or the general social climate
of liberalism or conservatism. Such events affect the people living
through them, although their effect is not the same for all age groups.

These events are difficult, if not impossible, to predict ahead of
time, but once they occur, we can predict that they will influence the developmental tasks of a particular generation. For the generation going
to college in the late 1960s and the early 1970s, for example, identifying
one's stand on the Vietnam war became a socially expected task. One
consequence of these normative historical influences is that we must expect that some developmental tasks will differ for different generations
and that historical events outside of colleges and universities will affect

the needs and concerns of students. In particular, those issues that may have been critical for us to think through as students may seem outdated and irrelevant to a new generation.

Non-Normative Life Influences. Baltes, Reese, and Lipsitt (1980) point to non-normative life events that influence development. These environmental and biological events do not occur in any predictable pattern for most individuals. Rather, they are the unique occurrences that may present a person with new, unexpected, and sometimes overwhelming developmental issues. Examples of such events would be a death in a family, illness, or job loss. The impact of such events may depend on their timing, intensity, duration, and prior expectations about their occurrence.

When events such as these happen, they can influence how an individual tackles the tasks that are normally expected of his or her age group. These events can provide an impetus for further social-cognitive development and for tackling normative age-related tasks with new vigor, or they can lead to stagnation and regression because they overwhelm the individual's ability to cope with normal environmental demands. When faced with such non-normative life events, students may need special support from student affairs staff members, so that the experiences do not retard normal development.

Normative Environmental Influences. Although normative environmental influences were not discussed by Baltes, Reese, and Lipsitt, it is important to note that certain environments may make task demands on the groups exposed to them. This may be particularly critical for understanding developmental concerns of college students that are not common among noncollege populations of a similar age. For example, the college environment requires that all students develop certain intellectual skills (such as writing, test taking, studying). As a consequence, Astin (1977) and Chickering (1969) have documented a consistent concern with intellectual competency among college populations. Developing intellectual competency is essential if students are to remain in college and is, therefore, a developmental task that requires considerable time and energy.

Normative Age-Graded Developmental Tasks

Because normative age-graded developmental tasks are by definition closely associated with chronological age, older students should be expected to have different concerns and needs than younger ones.

For purposes of illustration, the following discussion will focus on the age-related tasks of the traditional-aged college student.

The reader should note that, in general, developmental tasks are less specifically defined than social-cognitive developmental sequences. This is particularly true for the period after the early twenties. Little is known about the developmental tasks of young, middle-aged, and older adults, and what is known is almost exclusively limited to men. For some initial research in this area, the reader should consult Sheehy (1976), Levinson (1978), Vaillant (1977), and Neugarten (1968).

The traditional-aged college student is both at the end of adolescence and at the beginning of young adulthood. As a consequence, the developmental tasks associated with college students overlap with the other two periods. Many will enter college without having completed the developmental tasks of adolescence, while others will be ready to embark on those associated with the older group.

The primary developmental task of adolescence has been identified by Erikson (1968) as establishing an identity. Many of the vectors Chickering (1969) specified as critical to college student development can also be understood as subcomponents of the identity process. These include developing independence, identifying areas of competence, and sexual identification. Others (Havighurst, 1972) have emphasized the importance of making an initial career choice as part of establishing an identity.

Two aspects of the college environment emphasize the importance of making an initial career choice. First, time in college is limited. If students do not go on for further education, most must establish an independent source of income. In either case, there is environmental pressure to make a decison that involves an occupational choice. Most colleges require students to choose a major, which may also have strong occupational implications. In other words, the college environment is set up in such a way that initial career choice is strongly expected.

Erikson (1968) pointed to intimacy as the critical task of the young adult years. Havighurst (1972) added the following: selecting a mate, learning to live with a partner, starting a family, managing a household, getting started in an occupation, and establishing a social group. Some of these may be seen as components of the more general intimacy issue. Others are independent of it.

Many individuals begin to focus on these tasks in college. In addition to sexual maturation, there is considerable social pressure to identify a special social partner. Note, for example, the number of social activities that require students to attend with a date. As a consequence, knowing how to establish social relationships is a primary concern for the college student.

Implications

There are several implications of this complex developmental task model for student affairs professionals.

The majority of traditional-aged college students will be concerned about issues of identity, occupational choice, and interpersonal relationships. Because of the normative influences of the university environment, most students, no matter what their age, will have questions about their intellectual competence.

Because college falls at the end of adolescence and the beginning of adulthood, some students will be completing the tasks of adolescence. At the same time, there will be environmental pressure to accomplish the tasks of young adulthood. Many will be entering into special interpersonal relationships without having a mature identity through which to relate to the other person or on which to base the choice of a partner.

There will be considerable variability between individuals in the normative age-related tasks they have accomplished, especially between younger students and nontraditional ones. It may be important and helpful for student affairs professionals to assess how far along students are in accomplishing normative age-related tasks. There may be particular skills for some students that need remediation. In other areas, they may merely need support as they tackle new challenges.

Social-Cognitive Structure and Developmental Tasks

In the prior two sections of this chapter, two models of development have been mapped. In the first section, sequences of increasingly complex and abstract concepts of the world were described. These included logic, knowledge, morality, self, and relationships. While college students evolve increasingly complex and differentiated categories in each of these areas, development is not complete in the undergraduate years.

The second section dealt with developmental tasks. These tasks are the roles, attitudes, and skills that individuals need to develop as a consequence of environmental pressures and biological changes. Individuals may be influenced by normative as well as non-normative events.

Clearly, there are apparent overlaps in the issues addressed by the two models. This section will focus on how these two developmental processes are related in any single person. What is most important to note is that, despite environmental and biological pressures to accomplish certain tasks, college students will approach them with varying degrees of cognitive complexity. While in most cases their ability to deal with issues complexly will increase during the college years, their reasoning processes will not be fully developed. Thus, while there is pressure to make career decisions, for example, the categories the individual has available to think through the issues will not be fully mature. Both Knefelkamp and Slepitza (1976) and Welfel (1982) have traced the implications of cognitive development for career decision making. They suggest that some students may be operating with simple, absolutist concepts of career. For them, making a decision about a career exists only to the extent that they expect to find an absolutely true answer. They assume an authority will tell them what it it. As students develop more complex categories, they begin to understand that any career decision might be right or wrong. At the same time, they are bewildered about how to make the "right" decision, since they can no longer depend on authorities to give it. At a higher level of cognitive complexity, they begin to see that many careers may be legitimate possibilities, depending on the combination of skills and interests they wish to emphasize. The highest level of career decision making presupposes an integrated concept of self and an understanding of the probabilistic way data allow one to make judgments. It is only at this point that they are able to integrate what they previously perceived as diverse aspects of career choice into an integrated whole.

Few data are available on the relationship between cognitive complexity and career choice. Touchton and others (1977) report that most of the college students they studied used absolutist concepts of career choice. After an intense developmental course in career decision making, students used more complex concepts, but no student moved to the highest level.

One consequence of the need to accomplish important developmental tasks with incomplete social-cognitive maturity is that students find themselves in a precarious developmental bind. They must make a decision about a college major and about a career, but they do not have fully developed cognitive categories in order to do so. Students face similar binds when they are faced with establishing a sex-role identity or making a commitment to a relationship.

Conclusions

In the prior sections, I have argued that college students, both young and old, are developing increasingly complex and differentiated concepts of logic, knowledge, self, relationships, and morality. These conceptual networks are important because they provide the framework through which the individual understands the world around him or her, the nature of problem solving, relationships with others, and himself or herself. While these concepts change and become more complex and complete in the college years, it is unlikely that fully mature concepts in any of these areas develop until the middle to late twenties. Development that requires reorganizations of thought patterns takes place slowly. As a consequence, social-cognitive models should be understood as measuring and describing epocal changes, not fine-grained ones. Those who expect movement over several levels during the college years will probably be disappointed.

Little is known about the fine-grained quantitative changes that take place between the qualitative shifts in reasoning style represented by different levels. In addition, while it is known (Rest, 1981) that the college environment plays a large role in facilitating development, data on the specifics of this process are minimal. Both are issues that merit further investigation. Such investigations may require assessment instruments that are more sensitive to fine-grained changes than those that are currently available.

By contrast, developmental task models point to smaller, more specific changes in knowledge, attitudes, and roles that individuals need in order to face the challenges that growing older poses. In general, these tasks will differ for younger traditional-aged students and older students returning to school in their thirties, forties, and fifties. All groups will, however, face the developmental tasks imposed by the institution itself, such as developing intellectual competence. Clearly, student affairs professionals could play an important role in identifying task areas in which students have skill deficits and offering them remedial help.

These two models together provide a framework for understanding the changes, both qualitative and quantitative, that college students are making. In addition, they suggest that traditional-aged undergraduates, at least, are faced with a developmental double bind. These students are involved in the transition from the tasks of adolescence to the tasks of adulthood. As a consequence, they are pressed by parents, advisors, and peers to make decisions about careers, majors, and partners that may critically affect their future. At the same time, their concepts of self, relationships, and knowledge may leave them legitimately without a firm basis for making such decisions. Decisions must be made, however, even without a fully mature concept of self or even without understanding how data can justify a "best guess"!

From this perspective, one of the most critical roles that student affairs professionals may need to play with college students is to help them understand that they are not "finished products" when they leave college. Their identities will continue to form and their understanding of relationships will continue to change. They must understand that the decisions they make in college may need to be re-evaluated as their understanding of themselves and the world around them continues to evolve.

References

Arlin, P. K. "Cognitive Development in Adulthood: A Fifth Stage?" *Developmental Psychology,* 1975, *11,* 602–606.

Astin, A. W. *Four Critical Years: Effects of College on Beliefs, Attitudes, and Knowledge.* San Francisco: Jossey-Bass, 1977.

Baltes, P. B., Reese, H. W., and Lipsitt, L. P. "Life-Span Developmental Psychology." In M. R. Rosenzweig and L. W. Porter (Eds.), *Annual Review of Psychology.* Palo Alto, Calif.: Annual Reviews, 1980.

Brabeck, M. M. K. "The Relationship Between Critical Thinking Skills and Development of Reflective Judgment Among Adolescent and Adult Women." Unpublished doctoral dissertation, University of Cincinnati, 1980.

Broughton, J. "Development of Concepts of Self, Mind, Reality, and Knowledge." In W. Damon (Ed.), *New Directions for Child Development: Social Cognition,* no. 1. San Francisco: Jossey-Bass, 1978.

Chickering, A. W. *Education and Identity.* San Francisco: Jossey-Bass, 1969.

Colby, A. "Evolution of a Moral Development Theory." In W. Damon (Ed.), *New Directions for Child Development: Moral Development,* no. 2. San Francisco: Jossey-Bass, 1978.

Cooney, W. W., and Selman, R. L. "Children's Use of Social Conceptions." In W. Damon (Ed.), *New Directions for Child Development: Social Cognition,* no. 1. San Francisco: Jossey-Bass, 1978.

Davis, J. R. *Going to College.* Boulder, Colo.: Westview, 1977.

Drum, D. "Understanding Student Development." In W. H. Morrill and J. C. Hurst (Eds.), *Dimensions of Intervention for Student Development.* New York: Wiley, 1980.

Emmerich, W. "Personality Development and Concepts of Structure." *Child Development,* 1968, *39* (4), 671–686.

Erikson, E. H. *Childhood and Society.* New York: Norton, 1963.

Erikson, E. H. *Identity: Youth and Crisis.* New York: Norton, 1968.

Fischer, K. W. "A Theory of Cognitive Development: The Control and Construction of Hierarchies of Skills." *Psychological Review,* 1980, *87* (6), 477–531.

Fischer, K. W., Hand, H. H., and Russell, S. L. "The Development of Abstractions in Adolescence and Adulthood." In M. Commons (Ed.), *Beyond Formal Operations.* New York: Praeger, forthcoming.

Fischer, K. W., and Lazerson, A. "Cognitive Development in Adulthood." Unpublished manuscript, Department of Psychology, University of Denver, 1981.

Gilligan, C., and Murphy, J. M. "Development from Adolescence to Adulthood: The Philosopher and the Dilemma of the Fact." In D. Kuhn (Ed.), *New Directions for Child Development: Intellectual Development Beyond Childhood,* no. 5. San Francisco: Jossey-Bass, 1979.

Harvey, D. J., Hunt, D. E., and Schroder, H. M. *Conceptual Systems and Personality Organization.* New York: Wiley, 1961.

Hauser, S. T. "Loevinger's Model and Measure of Ego Development: A Critical Review." *Psychological Bulletin,* 1976, *83* (5), 928–955.

Havighurst, R. J. *Developmental Tasks and Education.* New York: McKay, 1972.

Heath, D. *Growing Up in College.* San Francisco: Jossey-Bass, 1968.

44

Heath, R. *The Reasonable Adventurer.* Pittsburgh, Pa.: University of Pittsburgh Press, 1964.

Inhelder, B., and Piaget, J. *The Growth of Logical Thinking.* London: Routledge & Kegan Paul, 1958.

King, P. M. "The Development of Reflective Judgment and Formal Operational Thinking in Adolescents and Young Adults." *Dissertation Abstracts International,* 1977, *38,* 723A.

King, P. M. "William Perry's Theory of Intellectual and Ethical Development." In L. Knefelkamp, C. Widick, and C. Parker (Eds.), *New Directions for Student Services: Applying New Developmental Findings,* no. 4. San Francisco: Jossey-Bass, 1978.

King, P. M., Kitchener, K. S., Davison, M. L., Parker, C., and Wood, P. K. "The Justification of Beliefs in Young Adults: A Longitudinal Study." *Human Development,* *26,* forthcoming.

Kitchener, K. S., and King, P. M. "Reflective Judgment: Concepts of Justification and Their Relationship to Age and Education." *Journal of Applied Developmental Psychology,* 1981, *2* (2), 89–116.

Kitchener, K. S., and Kitchener, R. F. "The Development of Natural Rationality: Can Formal Operations Account for It?" In J. S. Meacham and N. R. Santilli (Eds.), *Social Development in Youth: Structure and Content.* Basel, Switz.: Karger, 1981.

Kitchener, K. S., King, P. M., Davison, M. L., Parker, C., and Wood, P. K. "A Longitudinal Study of Moral and Ego Development in Young Adults." Unpublished manuscript, School of Education, University of Denver, 1982.

Knefelkamp, L., and Slepitza, R. L. "A Cognitive-Developmental Model of Career Development: An Adaptation of the Perry Scheme." *Counseling Psychologist,* 1976, *6* (3), 53–58.

Kohlberg, L. "Moral Stages and Moralization: The Cognitive Developmental Approach." In T. Lickona (Ed.), *Moral Development and Behavior.* New York: Holt, Rinehart and Winston, 1976.

Kohlberg, L. "Revisions in the Theory and Practice of Moral Development." In W. Damon (Ed.), *New Directions for Child Development: Moral Development,* no. 2. San Francisco: Jossey-Bass, 1978.

Lawrence, J. A. "Moral Judgment Intervention Studies Using the Defining Issues Test." *Journal of Moral Education,* 1980, *9,* 178–191.

Lerner, R. M. *Concepts and Theories of Human Development.* Reading, Mass.: Addison-Wesley, 1976.

Levinson, D., Darrow, C., Klein, E., Levinson, M., and McKee, B. *The Seasons of a Man's Life.* New York: Knopf, 1978.

Loevinger, J. *Ego Development: Conception and Theories.* San Francisco: Jossey-Bass, 1976.

Loevinger, J. "Construct Validity of the Sentence Completion Test of Ego Development." *Applied Psychological Measurement,* 1979, *3* (3), 281–311.

Loevinger, J., Wessler, R., and Redmore, C. *Measuring Ego Development.* Vol. I. *Construction and Use of a Sentence Completion Test.* San Francisco: Jossey-Bass, 1970.

Marcia, J. E. "Identity in Adolescence." In J. Adelson (Ed.), *Handbook of Adolescent Psychology.* New York: Wiley, 1980.

Mason, K. (Ed.). "Effects of Developmental Instruction on the Development of Cognitive Complexity, Locus of Control, and Empathy in Beginning Counseling Graduate Students." Unpublished master's thesis, University of Maryland, 1978.

Mines, R. A. "Levels of Intellectual Development and Associated Critical Thinking Skills in Young Adults." Unpublished doctoral dissertation, University of Iowa, 1980.

Neimark, E. D. "Intellectual Development During Adolescence." In F. D. Horowitz (Ed.), *Review of Child Development Research.* Chicago: University of Chicago Press, 1975.

Neimark, E. D. "Current Status of Formal Operations Research." *Human Development,* 1979, *22,* 60–67.

Neugarten, B. L. "Adult Personality: Toward a Psychology of the Life Cycle." In B. L. Neugarten (Ed.), *Middle Age and Aging.* Chicago: University of Chicago Press, 1968.

Parker, C., Widick, C., Knefelkamp, L. "Why Bother with Theory?" In L. Knefelkamp, C. Widick, C. Parker (Eds.), *New Directions for Student Services: Applying New Developmental Findings,* no. 4. San Francisco: Jossey-Bass, 1978.

Perry, W. G. *Forms of Intellectual and Ethical Development in the College Years.* New York: Holt, Rinehart and Winston, 1970.

Piaget, J. "Piaget's Theory." In P. H. Mussen (Ed.), *Carmichael's Manual of Child Psychology.* New York: Wiley, 1970.

Piaget, J. "Intellectual Evolution from Adolescence to Adulthood." *Human Development,* 1972, *15,* 1–12.

Rest, J. R. *Development in Judging Moral Issues.* Minneapolis: University of Minnesota Press, 1979.

Rest, J. R. "The Impact of Higher Education on Moral Judgment Development." Paper presented at the American Education Research Association National Convention, Los Angeles, April 1981.

Riegal, K. F. *Foundations of Dialectical Psychology.* New York: Academic Press, 1979.

Sanford, N. *Self and Society.* New York: Atherton Press, 1966.

Schaie, K. W., and Geiwitz, J. *Adult Development and Aging.* Boston: Little, Brown, 1982.

Schmidt, J. A., and Davison, M. "Does College Matter? Reflective Judgment: How Student Tackle the Tough Question." *Moral Education Forum,* 1981, pp. 2–14.

Sheehy, G. *Passages.* New York: Dutton, 1976.

Shoff, S. P. "The Significance of Age, Sex, and Type of Education on the Development of Reasoning in Adults." Unpublished doctoral dissertation, University of Utah, 1979.

Stephenson, B. W., and Hunt, C. "Intellectual and Ethical Development: A Dualistic Curriculum and Intervention for College Students." *Counseling Psychologist,* 1977, *6* (4), 39–42.

Strange, C., and King, P. M. "Intellectual Development and Its Relationship to Maturation in the College Years." *Journal of Applied Developmental Psychology,* 1977, *6* (4), 39–42.

Tomlinson-Keasey, C. "Formal Operations in Females from Eleven to Fifty-Four Years of Age." *Developmental Psychology,* 1972, *6,* 364.

Touchton, J. G., Wertheimer, L. C., Cornfeld, J. L., and Harrison, K. H. "Career Planning and Decision Making: A Developmental Approach to the Classroom." *Counseling Psychologist,* 1977, *6* (4), 42–47.

Valliant, G. E. *Adaptation to Life.* Boston: Little, Brown, 1977.

Welfel, E. R. "The Development of Reflective Judgment: Implications for Career Counseling of College Students." *Personnel and Guidance Journal,* 1982, *61,* 17–21.

Whitbourne, S. K., and Weinstock, C. S. *Adult Development.* New York: Holt, Rinehart and Winston, 1979.

Widick, C., Knefelkamp, L., and Parker, C. "The Counselor as Developmental Instructor." *Counselor Education and Supervision,* 1975, *14,* 286–296.

Wohlwill, J. F. *The Study of Behavioral Development.* New York: Academic Press, 1973.

*Karen Strohm Kitchener is assistant professor and training
director for the counseling psychology program located in the
School of Education at the University of Denver. She is
currently a member of the executive council of the American
College Student Personnel Association. She has been involved
in a six-year longitudinal study of social-cognitive development
in college students and young adults and has written on the
development of concepts of justification and their importance
for adult reasoning.*

Student affairs professionals talk about student development
a great deal but do very little to document that the
programs we devise actually help students grow and change.
Explanations for this interesting paradox are reviewed
and some possible solutions are presented.

Critical Issues in the Assessment of Student Development

Gary R. Hanson

The student affairs profession must confront a very interesting paradox in the 1980s. The paradox is that we philosophize, conceptualize, and theorize about student development, but we do very little to document how students change while in college. Let us consider the nature of the paradox in more detail. The student affairs profession has been committed to the development of students for a very long time; our historical roots can be traced back to the early colonial colleges (Fenske, 1980; Miller, Chapter One, this volume; Saddlemire, 1980). Throughout our history, we have made philosophical statements about the importance of educating the whole student (American Council on Education, 1937, 1949; Council of Student Personnel Associations, 1975). Also, in the last decade alone, we have witnessed a literal explosion of theoretical writings regarding human development (Drum, 1980; Knefelkamp, Widick, and Parker, 1978; Morrill and Hurst, 1980; Rodgers, 1980). With a long-term commitment to the philosophy of student development and a solid theoretical foundation for conceptualizing how students change, should not the student affairs profession be engaged in the practice of student development? We are. Miller and Prince (1976) describe a number of innovative programs from throughout the higher

G. R. Hanson (Ed.). *Measuring Student Development.* New Directions
for Student Services, no. 20. San Francisco: Jossey-Bass, December 1982.

education community that attempt to implement our philosophy and theory. One need only examine our professional literature to find descriptions of many, many student service programs designed to facilitate college student development. What we do not find is a systematic attempt to assess student development, to document that our programs work. Neither do we find empirical studies that simply describe students in developmental terms. Interestingly, many of the theoretical writings have been based on very solid research evidence, both clinical and quantitative in nature. Somehow, once theories are developed and go through several stages of revision, further assessment seems to decline. For example, in checking the professional literature from 1970 through mid-1982, only a small handful of empirical studies, less than ten, were reported in the literature that documented any of the theoretical writings of Perry (1970), Kohlberg (1971), Loevinger (1966), Heath (1968), Erikson (1963), or any other theorists. Why is there so little documentation of student development in our professional literature? With a student development philosophy embedded in the very beginnings of higher education in the United States and with a rich conceptual base, is it not strange that our profession has done so little to assess student development, to document what we believe so strongly and practice so arduously?

The purpose of this chapter is to examine some of the critical issues that make the assessment of student development difficult. Identifying and discussing these critical issues will make possible a better understanding of how to proceed with the assessment of student change. Before we can do a good job of measuring student development, we must take a critical look at some of the barriers that prohibit us from assessing students in developmental terms. The next section of this chapter looks at a variety of explanations for why the student affairs profession has done so much talking about student development but so little assessment. After reviewing some of the reasons why assessment is not taking place, a number of solutions to these issues will be proposed.

Why No Assessment?

There are many reasons why student affairs professionals fail to assess student development. Possible explanations range from competing political priorities to inadequate graduate training to problems of definition to difficult measurement processes. In analyzing these possible reasons, no one issue seems to dominate the others. Most likely, a combination of problems results in student affairs professionals not even trying to assess how, when, and why students change as a result of their college experience.

Multiple Definitions of Student Development. Ten to fifteen years ago, student affairs professionals were just beginning to read widely the literature of human development, and the definitions of student development that followed were vague and nebulous. Since then, graduate training programs have increased the number of courses that include readings related to the developmental process. Today, on the other hand, a frequent complaint of students and practitioners alike is that there are too many different theories of development. While there are several excellent summaries (Drum, 1980; Knefelkamp, Widick, and Parker, 1978; Morrill and Hurst, 1980; Rodgers, 1980), the sheer volume of theoretical writings makes it difficult for both the new professional as well as the experienced practitioner to assess students according to these theoretical models. Many of the theoretical writings are based on clinical interviews and case studies. While this method of theory development provides a rich conceptual framework, few of the theories are based on assessment instruments that are easy to use and understand. Kitchener points out in an earlier chapter of this volume that some of the important dimensions of student development have no corresponding assessment procedures available whatsoever. She specifically points out that Drum (1980) has identified several very important dimensions of student development for which no assessment procedures have been developed. As a result of the many different definitions of student development, practitioners are most likely to use theoretical models for which assessment procedures are readily available. Hence, Chickering's (1969) theory of college student development has received much attention because the Student Development Task Inventory (Winston, Miller, and Prince, 1981) is an instrument that is easy to use. Other instruments are being developed to measure other theoretical dimensions of student development but are in a less advanced stage of refinement.

Failing to Identify Possible Uses Before Assessment. A major problem in the assessment of student development is the failure to identify what uses to make of the data. All too often, assessment projects are started without giving adequate forethought to how the data will be used and for what purposes the assessment will be made. The assessment of student development can be made for a variety of reasons, and the selection of instruments, as well as the utilization of the data, will vary depending on what particular use was intended. For example, Lenning (1980) identifies eight major uses of assessment data. The uses that seem most important for student affairs are description, evaluation, planning, and monitoring.

As Knefelkamp, Widick, and Parker (1978) point out, we need to understand who the college student is in developmental terms. What changes occur and what do these changes look like? Few colleges assess students in developmental terms when they first enter as freshmen and, not surprisingly, have trouble documenting what changes occur over the next several years they spend on campus. Think about the situation on your campus. Can you document what percentage of freshmen think in a manner described by the Perry (1970) stage of dualism, multiplicity, or relativism? Do seniors on your campus think differently than freshmen? An important point to remember in developing descriptive uses of student development measures is that they provide a baseline of knowledge on which to initiate your student service programs.

Another descriptive use is to help students understand themselves in developmental terms. Miller and Prince (1976) suggest that the measurement of student development be done in conjunction with the student. That is, the student must be an agent in the measurement process. The assessment data have little or no meaning if students cannot use the data to better understand themselves and what they must do to change. Again, the descriptive use provides a baseline of information — in this case, for the student to begin the process of self-understanding.

The second major use of student development data is to monitor the process of change. After assessing the developmental status of students we need to follow and monitor their progress through the use of student development transcripts, as described by Brown, 1980; Brown and Citrin, 1977; and Brown and DeCoster, 1982. With a developmental transcript, students, faculty, and administrators can make judgments about specific areas of accomplishment, identify areas for further effort, and describe to others what development has occurred within a given period of time. By monitoring the developmental status of students, program administrators can begin to link the way in which students change to certain program efforts. Programs can then be modified to retain those elements that lead to a positive change in students and to eliminate those program elements that have little or no impact.

Another important use of assessment data based on student development is for planning purposes. One way to facilitate student development is to intentionally plan for the change to occur. Not only are descriptive data, mentioned previously, important, but we must also describe the process and course the development is likely to follow. Describing student development may take one assessment procedure, while the assessment of the developmental process may take a very different kind of assessment procedure. The use of both types of data — descriptive and process — is particularly important in planning the delivery of services and in designing instructional curriculum (Fried, 1981).

Finally, the assessment of student development can be used to evaluate our educational efforts. We hope students change, and we spend no small amount of effort to see that they do. Rarely, however, do we collect any evidence on how well we have done. Using measures of student development for evaluative purposes requires that we systematically relate what was done within a specific program, activity, or classroom to the way in which students change. We need to find out what aspects of the program facilitated a given type of change in the way students think or behave. For example, if a residence hall director wanted to evaluate whether the social programming for a given floor helped students develop a greater sense of autonomy, data could be collected before and after the programming took place for both the floor in question and for another floor in which no programming took place. Two types of data would then have to be maintained: (1) when, where, and how the program activities took place and (2) the nature and magnitude of how the students changed. With these data, an evaluation could be made regarding which aspects of the program were related to the change in students. The evaluation would be especially effective if multiple assessments of student autonomy could be made. As different aspects of the program were implemented, the change in students could be monitored to see which activities resulted in the desired change.

Competing Priorities Within the Institution. One of the reasons very little assessment of student development occurs is that it must take place within the political arena of higher education. While Brown (1972) encouraged our profession to collaborate with faculty in the academic arena, one practical reality is that we compete very directly not only for limited resources but for the very goals of higher education. While the student affairs profession subscribes to the developmental perspective, not everyone in higher education does. The debate regarding the relative emphasis between cognitive development and other important dimensions has been evident for a long time. Most recently, the Carnegie Commission (1973) recognized the importance of educating the whole student but emphasized that colleges should foster cognitive development; individuals should take the responsibility for development of their social, emotional, and personal skills. As Feldman (1972) pointed out a decade ago, some of the goals of higher education are not only indifferent to the developmental perspective but are outright antagonistic to it. If primary importance is placed on the socializing function of higher education, little attention or effort is given to how students change over the course of their college experience. This competing framework assumes that college certifies students for certain social and occupational positions in the world, channels them in these directions, and, to some extent, assures them of entrance into such positions. This orientation pays little attention to the personality, attitudinal, and behavioral changes of students as they move through college. That students assume new social and occupational roles as a result of attending college may, in fact, hinder their personal growth and development. Assuming these new roles says nothing about the process or nature of that change but merely that a qualitatively different status has been achieved sometimes at a considerable cost to the further development of the student.

Traditionally, student affairs professionals have not fared well in the philosophical debates regarding the goals of higher education. While many colleges claim their interest in the development of students in their college catalogues, the allocation of resources to ensure that such development takes place is frequently missing. As Mines shows in another chapter in this volume, assessment of student development is time consuming and expensive. If a college president has to decide to buy more books for a library, fund a sabbatical for an important faculty member, or study how students change in college, what do you think the president will pursue? Even when the institution subscribes to the developmental perspective, the allocation of funds will meet considerable resistance from other competing priorities. Rarely will staff time, resources, and money be provided to do the very kind of assessment that could document whether or not and to what extent college students change as a result of attending college.

Complex Administration and Scoring. Most of the instruments used to measure student development require the administration of stimulus materials in a structured interview and expert judges to rate a student's response. The time required to collect data from an individual will vary depending on the complexity of his or her responses, but an hour or more is often required. Once the data are collected, two or more raters are asked to review the data and make judgments regarding the level or category of the student. This scoring procedure may take another hour or more to complete, sometimes much longer if the two raters can not agree. Graduate students and researchers using these assessment techniques will appreciate the amount of time and level of training it takes to achieve a satisfactory level of rating consistent with the expert judges. Individuals unwilling to take the time to learn the appropriate scoring procedures may have to pay others to collect and score the data, but the cost may be very high: Three to five dollars per individual is not uncommon. That the assessment of student development does not occur is not surprising; it is time consuming and expensive!

Not all student development assessment techniques require a lot of time and money. The Student Development Task Inventory (SDTI), developed by Winston, Miller, and Prince (1981), is one exception. The instrument can be scored by students in about one-half hour or less. Other experimental assessment instruments are being developed that also hold promise for easier administration and scoring, but for the last five years the assessment of student development has definitely been held in check by cumbersome, if necessary, administration and scoring procedures.

Different Assessment Methods Produce Different Results. Student development can be assessed using a variety of techniques but, unfortunately, different methods produce different results. For example, Rest (1976) identified four different kinds of measures to collect data about Kohlberg's (1971) stages of moral development. One method asked individuals to rate each statement on a Likert-type scale to indicate how much they liked the statement or how forceful or persuasive they found its arguments. This procedure is called a *preference* measure. Another common technique is to ask individuals to paraphrase or recapitulate a statement or demonstrate understanding of a statement by drawing out its implications, a procedure called *comprehension recapitulation.* A third technique asks individuals to read a statement and then select from a list of other statements the one that comes closest in meaning to the original. This technique is called *comprehension by matching.* A fourth technique asks individuals to read statements about moral development and then at a later time reproduce them. Rest (1976) points out that these four different assessment methods elicit different kinds of data. Each method assesses a different level of acquisition of an idea. For example, a person can recognize and discriminate and thus prefer an idea before he or she can paraphrase it or before the idea can be spontaneously produced in response to a story or dilemma. Hence, the same individual may be located at different stages of moral development depending on the type of assessment technique used. Rest maintains that many individuals fully comprehend statements at higher stages than the predominant stage that they spontaneously use on the Kohlberg free response interview and, furthermore, that most individuals prefer statements at a stage higher than that typically used or the stage they are most likely to understand.

Multidimensional Nature of Development. Nearly all theories of student development assume that development occurs across several dimensions. Drum (1980) identifies seven important dimensions along which college students may experience change over the course of their college career. Lenning (1980) has developed a taxonomy of more than fifty student characteristics subject to change as a result of students' attending college. When assessing student development, one must carefully select the primary dimensions and search for the necessary instruments and procedures to measure those aspects of development.

Few instruments are designed to measure multiple dimensions of student development. At best, any given instrument may measure several dimensions from a given theory but not all of them. For example, the Student Development Task Inventory (Winston, Miller, and Prince, 1981) measures five subtasks out of the possible nine proposed by the Chickering (1969) theory on which it is based. Many instruments only intend to measure a single aspect of development and anyone interested in monitoring the development of students across several dimensions may have to use two, three, or more different instruments with a corresponding increase in time, effort, and money to collect the data.

Consistency of Response. The assessment of student development implies that we can observe patterns of behavior or thought that are consistent over short periods of time but are subject to change over longer time periods. Without a certain level of consistency on the part of individuals, we would have nothing to measure except seemingly random behavior or thought patterns. If people were consistent all the time, we would have no change or development. A central issue in the assessment of student development is measuring those thoughts and behaviors that form patterns that are sufficiently stable to suggest important psychological constructs while at the same time having sufficient sensitivity built into the instrument to detect significant change when it does occur. Inconsistency may arise when individuals are in periods of transition between developmental stages or levels. In these periods of transition, responses to assessment instruments are often unstable and confused and the process of reaching the next developmental stage or level seems to be gradual rather than abrupt. Responses may waver between one assessment level and another, making it difficult to accurately classify the appropriate developmental status.

Inconsistency in assessment may also arise from several possible sources: differences in stimulus materials, the manner of presentation of the relevant information, and the amount of irrelevant information the individual uses to make judgments. For example, if a single story or a single test item is used to assess the general moral judgment level of an individual, very different levels of assessment will occur across individuals because of inconsistent levels of response by any one individual. Also, whenever comparisons are made among individuals, the same set of test stimuli should be employed under standardized conditions. If somewhat different stories are used or individuals are interviewed with different probe questions or under different response conditions, then inconsistent responses will make comparisons impossible.

Using qualitative descriptions to summarize the developmental status of an individual may be inappropriate because the responses of individuals are not consistent enough to be classified accurately into any one stage. Rather, the results of an assessment should be summarized not as a stage category but as a probability statement that the responses occur with a particular frequency in any given stage. Instead of talking about a Stage 4 individual according to Kohlberg's (1971) theory, we should talk about an individual with a 40 percent probability of a Stage 4 response, a 20 percent probability of a Stage 3 response, a 10 percent Stage 5 response, and so forth. The latter method is more statistically accurate but certainly more cumbersome for the practitioner.

Accuracy of Assessment. Assessment data are useful only to the extent that the accuracy of what is measured matches the kind of decision that must be made using the data. One of the reasons more assessment of student development is not done is that our assessment techniques do not provide enough detailed information with sufficient accuracy to make good decisions on how to design educational curriculum, student service programs, or provide individual counseling. How much accuracy is necessary to design an academic course that takes into consideration the way in which individuals think as defined by Perry's (1970) theory of cognitive development? Would you need an instrument that could assess whether they used a dualistic mode of thinking versus a multiplistic mode? Or would you need to make finer distinctions within the dualistic mode? An instrument that provided scores that only allowed you to make gross judgments from one major developmental stage to another would do you little good if your intent were to diagnose the modes of thinking within a freshman class, most of whom were known to fall within the dualistic mode of thinking. Similar problems arise when trying to use developmental assessment data to plan student service programs or individual counseling. In general, the more likely the data is to be used to make decisions about individuals, the more accurate the assessment procedure must be. The consequences of making a judgmental error with individuals are more severe than making an error about a group of people and, hence, the data should be more accurate. Assessment instruments and procedures must be evaluated carefully to fully understand the level of accuracy available for any given use of an instrument.

One indicator of the accuracy of an assessment instrument is the level of reliability obtained for a given assessment situation. The particular sample, setting, instructions, and instrument will influence the level of reliability that can be obtained. In general, if decisions are to be made about individuals, the reliability should be .9 or higher, while decisions about groups can be made with instruments with estimates of reliability in the .70 to .80 range.

Lack of Planning. One obvious reason why more assessment is not taking place is that little long-range planning includes the assessment of student development. As the chapter by Krone and Hanson in this volume suggests, the inclusion of student development assessment data must occur early in the planning process, long before steps are taken to implement the program itself. To make sure that the assessment occurs in a timely and useful fashion, it is necessary to plan to include the data collection as an integral part of an overall program or classroom experience. All too many times the need for a good assessment of student development will occur to the program planners well into the implementation of the program. By that time, it is much too late to go back and collect retrospective data about the developmental status of students. Questions must be asked about the kinds of data that will be needed, the kinds of decisions that need to be made, and how the data will be used once it is collected. Answers to these questions will determine the instrument to use, the possible sample to collect the data from and will force the planner to consider the eventual audience who will receive the data and what form they need to be in so the audience can make sense of them. Data that researchers or faculty find of the greatest interest may not necessarily be the kind of data that program administrators need to make decisions about costs, improvements, or terminations of certain program elements.

Few Guidelines for Selecting Instruments. Not only are there relatively few standardized assessment instruments for measuring student development but available guidelines for deciding which instruments to use for which purposes are almost nonexistent. Even when decisions are made about the type of data needed for a particular classroom or program use, translating those needs into a specific type of instrument is difficult. What levels of reliability are needed for the decision, and what levels does a given instrument yield under the assessment conditions for a particular project? Depending on the use you plan to make of the data, is predictive, concurrent, or construct validity of greatest importance? Does the instrument have evidence supporting each of these different kinds of validity? Another important consideration in the selection of an instrument is the total cost of the data collection. Some instruments are relatively inexpensive to administer but very expensive to score. Others have modest costs for both administration and scoring. Unfortunately, few instruments are inexpensive to administer and to score.

Inability to Use Assessment Results. The single most important reason why very little assessment of student development occurs is that most student affairs professionals do not know what to do with the data once they get it. The source of the problem is twofold: The data resulting from most assessment instruments are too abstract and removed from daily practice, and few professionals have the necessary training to use what is available or to develop new assessment procedures that are useful.

That the current generation of assessment instruments is abstract and theory-bound is understandable. The development of theory required instruments that would yield information to help refine the theory. Using information from these same instruments to guide practice is difficult because there is no direct link between the theory and what we must do to deliver student services or teach in the classroom. For example, knowing that a student's primary mode of thinking is classified at Perry's (1970) dualistic stage provides interesting information about *how* the student thinks and may be expected to progress to more complex modes of thought. Knowing that the student or a whole class of students uses this mode of thinking gives relatively little information to the teacher about what or how to teach. Should students who use a dualistic mode of thinking be taught mathematics and history using the same strategies? Most student development assessment instruments simply do not provide information with enough precision to provide specific direction to programming or classroom activities.

Not knowing what to do with assessment results is also a function of inadequate training in our graduate programs. Minimal coursework should be provided for student affairs professionals in order that sound decisions be made regarding the selection and use of appropriate assessment instruments. More advanced training would be required for anyone interested in developing special instruments for local campus use. Even when graduate courses are taught in measurement and assessment procedures, little time is devoted to the presentation and dissemination of data, especially developmental data. Most graduate courses focus on the assessment of individual difference measures taken at one point in time, such as career interest inventories, personality measures, and academic aptitude tests. The special problems of dealing with the measurement, analysis, and reporting of growth data are not dealt with except in very advanced courses. As a result, very few individuals have a solid foundation in the assessment of student growth.

Few Informal Methods of Assessment. Lenning (1980) discussed formal and informal methods of assessment. Most of the instruments developed to date have been formal in nature, and almost no assessment procedures have been developed that rely on informal methods of assessment. Depending on the purpose of assessment, informal assessment techniques may be more than adequate, cost less, and be much simpler to administer, score, and interpret. One of the reasons there are few informal assessment instruments is that most developmental phenomena represent rather complex behavior or thought processes. Using checklists, unobtrusive measures, or simple rating scales will not allow the assessment of complex behavior such as the thought processes of students use in learning new material. Informal assessment methods may be useful in measuring growth and development in behavioral terms when developmental tasks or stages are the focus. One example is the Student Development Task Inventory (Winston, Miller, and Prince, 1981) which uses a relatively simple rating scale of student experience along several developmental task dimensions of Chickering's (1969) vectors of development.

New Directions for Assessment

The assessment of student development is in an infant stage of development. Very little assessment is done and most of it results in very crude measurement that is reported in difficult and abstract terms. That little use is made of these assessment results is not at all surprising. What needs to be done to incorporate the assessment of student development into the everyday practice of student service professionals? The assessment of student development must be redirected. The purpose of this section is to suggest some new directions we must pursue.

Simplify the Assessment Process. A distinction should be made between the use of assessment results to refine theoretical statements and the use of them for programming and service delivery. Data collection that involves the subjective judgments of expert raters will continue to play an important role in the development and refinement of developmental theory. These data provide a wealth of information about the process of development that would be difficult to obtain using any other kind of assessment methods. For programming, service delivery, and classroom use, however, the assessment of student development must be simplified. The collection of the data should take less time, should be easier to score, and the results should be expressed in the simplest terms possible.

More experimentation should be done with informal assessment techniques. Simple paper and pencil instruments need to be developed that could be self-scored by students. Checklists and rating sheets of critical student developmental tasks should be constructed and validated in order to make the evaluation of student service programs and classroom instruction easier to conduct. Good progress is being made in the use of simple assessment instruments with the student development transcripts described by Brown and DeCoster (1982). These instruments are used by students to monitor their own development and by faculty to aid in the academic advising process.

Reduce the Cost of Assessment. Most methods to assess student development are costly in terms of time and money. The assessment of a single individual may take several hours and cost up to $25.00 to administer and score. If we expect to see the assessment of student development done on a large scale, ways must be found to reduce the costs. Naturally, making the assessment instruments simpler to administer and score would be a step in the right direction. Almost no work is being done to develop computer-assisted assessment with student development assessment instruments in the way that administration and scoring is done for such well known instruments as the Minnesota Multiphasic Personality Inventory or the Strong-Campbell Interest Inventory. Once computer programs are developed and written — no small investment of time and money — the cost of scoring and administration per individual drops dramatically. Costs can also be lowered by developing instruments scored by the individuals who complete them, as is possible with the Student Development Task Inventory (Winston, Miller, and Prince, 1981) and many popular personality inventories. The advantage of self-scored assessment instruments is that the individual obtains immediate results. If the goal of the assessment is to increase the individual's awareness of his or her development, making the results available immediately may facilitate that understanding.

Assess Multiple Dimensions of Student Development. To recommend that assessment instruments be simplified and measure multiple dimensions of student development may sound contradictory. Two different aspects of the assessment process are involved, however. Administration and scoring refer to the process of data collection, while the assessment of multiple dimensions of student development refers to the content of what is being measured. A very simple construct could be measured by a very complex process — as is now being done in most student development instruments — or a very complex psychological construct or constructs can be measured using relatively simple assessment strategies. To increase the usefulness of our assessment techniques, we need to concentrate more on the latter and less on the former.

If the purpose of our assessment is to monitor, evaluate, plan, or describe student development and not to refine theory, then measuring multiple dimensions of development is crucial. We need to think of students in more complex terms — that they change in different ways at various times along a wide variety of growth dimensions. The programs we deliver undoubtedly do not have the same affect on the way students think, feel, and behave at different times in their lives. We should find out which programs and classroom activities influence which dimensions of growth, but to do that our assessment instruments must measure multiple dimensions of development.

Encourage Longitudinal Assessment Studies. To be valid, our assessment of student development must occur over a sufficient time period for the growth or change to take place. Likewise, the measurement of development implies that at least two and preferably more measurements must be taken before a judgment about the direction and nature of the development can be made. These two requirements demand that we plan the assessment process carefully and that it be done using a longitudinal design. Too many of the studies to validate student development instruments have relied on group differences using a cross-sectional design. The assumption is made that freshmen and seniors must differ on some developmental dimension and if an assessment instrument shows such a difference it must be valid. Such an assessment says nothing about whether or not the change actually occurred but only that two groups expected to differ did not obtain the same scores. Other factors correlated with a particular dimension of student development may have caused the difference in scores. For example, entering freshmen and graduating seniors would be expected to use different modes of thinking. The seniors probably reason from multiple perspectives and allow their values to influence their judgments, while freshmen may reason from a dualistic perspective and be influenced greatly by what others say. Theory suggests these two groups would obtain different scores, and they may well do so. However, if reading comprehension was important in the assessment process, the differences in the freshmen and senior scores may be the result of differences in reading ability, a skill learned during college and not due to developmental changes in the way these two groups of students think. A comparison of the two groups would say very little about development, but a longitudinal study that assessed freshmen in developmental terms, controlled for differences in reading ability, and then assessed the same students as seniors would stand a much better chance of detecting changes in the way students think. When evaluating the usefulness of student development assessment instruments, the evidence supporting the validity of the instrument must include studies using a longitudinal design.

Require Minimal Skills in Assessment Methodology. The assessment of student development will not be done if student affairs professionals do not know how to do it. Not every professional staff member needs to know the technical details of how to conduct an effective assessment, but all staff should know how to select assessment instruments appropriate to a given use, interpret the results of assessment instruments, and use the results to design effective student service programs or classroom activities. These minimal competencies are rarely taught in our current graduate training programs, and few staff development training programs emphasize the acquisition of these skills. They should. Without these minimal competencies as a basic foundation, student development assessment results will never be used to any degree outside of doctoral dissertation research.

Refine the Assessment of Student Development. The results obtained from most student development instruments provide a rough picture of the developmental status of an individual. Most of the scores are global and may only reflect a general stage or category of development that subsumes many important pieces of information about the ways in which the student feels, thinks, or behaves. Our assessment of student development must be refined to become more diagnostic in nature. To refine our instruments and assessment procedures, however, we need to know more about the why of student development. A closer link must be made between the constructs of student development and their antecedent causes.

The nature and direction this assessment must take is best illustrated with a practical example. If a classroom instructor wishes to stimulate students who use a mode of thinking characterized by Perry (1963) as dualistic to a mode characterized as multiplistic what kinds of information might be needed? The following questions represent only a few of the many kinds of information the instructor would find helpful:

- What teaching method or style challenges students who think in dualistic ways?
- Do all students who think in dualistic ways respond in the same manner to the instructor's teaching style?
- What causes some students to adopt a more complex mode of thinking?
- Why do some educational activities cause some students to try new ways of thinking and other students to hold firm?
- Do students who use a dualistic mode of thinking to solve math problems use the same mode of thinking to write English theme papers or make career decisions?
- Once new modes of thinking are adopted, what circumstances are likely to cause them to revert back to previous modes of thinking?
- How much change from one mode of thinking to another can be expected in a year, a semester, or a month?

These questions point to an assessment process or instrument that provides data about the developmental status of individuals, how

62

they change, when they change, and what conditions seem to influence the change. For such instruments or processes to work, a greater level of detail and accuracy of measurement is needed. In the future, measures of student development must provide information in enough detail to prescribe specific interventions.

Summary

A paradox does face the student affairs profession: We talk a great deal about the importance of student development but we do not know how and when or why students change during their college experience. We will never know unless we become more systematic in our assessment of student development. Numerous barriers were outlined in this chapter that make the assessment of student development difficult, but none of them is insurmountable. If we can refine the assessment instruments, make them less costly and easier to use, and train our professionals in what to do with the results, then we can plan and deliver our student services with greater confidence that we will have helped students grow and develop in the process.

References

American Council on Education. "The Student Personnel Point of View." *American Council on Education Studies*. (Series 1, vol. 1, no. 3.) Washington, D.C.: American Council on Education, 1937.

American Council on Education, "The Student Personnel Point of View." *American Council on Education Studies*. (Series 6, vol. 13, no. 13.) Washington, D.C.: American Council on Education, 1949.

Brown, R. D. *Student Development in Tomorrow's Higher Education: A Return to the Academy.* (Monograph no. 16.) Washington, D.C.: American College Personnel Monograph Series, 1972.

Brown, R. D. "The Student Development Educator Role." In U. Delworth and G. R. Hanson and Associates (Eds.), *Student Services: A Handbook for the Profession.* San Francisco: Jossey-Bass, 1980.

Brown, R. D., and Citrin, R. "A Student Development Transcript: Assumptions, Uses and Formats." *Journal of College Student Personnel*, 1977, *18*, 163–168.

Brown, R. D., and DeCoster, D. A. (Eds.) *New Directions for Student Services: Mentoring Transcript Systems for Promoting Student Growth*, no. 19. San Francisco: Jossey-Bass, 1982.

Carnegie Commission on Higher Education. *The Purposes and Performance of Higher Education in the United States.* New York: McGraw-Hill, 1973.

Chickering, A. *Education and Identity.* San Francisco: Jossey-Bass, 1969.

Council of Student Personnel Associations. "Student Development Services in Postsecondary Education." *Journal of College Student Personnel*, 1975, *16*, 524–528.

Drum, D. "Understanding Student Development." In W. Morrill and J. Hurst (Eds.), *Dimensions of Intervention for Student Development.* New York: Wiley, 1980.

Erikson, E. H. *Childhood and Society.* (2nd ed.) New York: W. W. Norton and Co., 1963.

Feldman, K. A. "Some Theoretical Approaches to the Study of Change and Stability of College Students." *Review of Educational Research,* 1972, *42,* 1–25.

Fenske, R. H. "Historical Foundations." In U. Delworth and G. R. Hanson and Associates (Eds.), *Student Services: A Handbook for the Profession.* San Francisco: Jossey-Bass, 1980.

Fried, J. "Education for Student Development." In J. Fried (Ed.), *New Directions for Student Services: Education for Student Development,* no. 15. San Francisco: Jossey-Bass, 1981.

Heath, D. *Growing Up in College.* San Francisco: Jossey-Bass, 1968.

Knefelkamp, L. L., Widick, C., and Parker, C. L. (Eds.). *New Directions for Student Services: Applying New Developmental Findings,* no. 4. San Francisco: Jossey-Bass, 1978.

Kohlberg L. "Stages of Moral Development." In C. M. Beck, B. S. Crittenden, and E. V. Sullivan (Eds.), *Moral Education.* Toronto: University of Toronto Press, 1971.

Lenning, O. T. "Assessment and Evaluation." In U. Delworth, G. R. Hanson, and Associates (Eds.), *Student Services: A Handbook for the Profession.* San Francisco: Jossey-Bass, 1980.

Loevinger, J. "The Meaning and Measurement of Ego Development." *American Psychologist,* 1966, *21,* 195–206.

Miller, T. K., and Prince, J. S. *The Future of Student Affairs: A Guide to Student Development for Tomorrow's Higher Education.* San Francisco: Jossey-Bass, 1976.

Morrill, W., and Hurst, J. C. (Eds.). *Dimensions of Interventions for Student Development.* New York: Wiley, 1980.

Perry, W. G. *Forms of Intellectual and Ethical Development in the College Years.* New York: Holt, Rinehart and Winston, 1970.

Rest, J. R. "New Approaches in the Assessment of Moral Development." In T. Lickona (Ed.), *Moral Development and Behavior.* New York: Holt, Rinehart, and Winston, 1976.

Rodgers, R. In D. Creamer (Ed.), *Student Development in Higher Education: Theories, Practices, and Future Directions.* Washington, D.C.: American College Personnel Association, 1980.

Saddlemire, G. L. "Professional Development." In U. Delworth and G. R. Hanson and Associates (Eds.), *Student Services: A Handbook for the Profession.* San Francisco: Jossey-Bass, 1980.

Winston, R. B., Miller, T. K., and Prince, J. S. *Assessing Student Development.* Athens, Ga.: Student Development Associates, 1981.

Gary R. Hanson is assistant dean of students at the University of Texas at Austin and is responsible for the student life studies area of the Office of the Dean of Students.

Existing student development assessment techniques are reviewed
and evaluated in terms of developmental assessment issues,
measurement methods, and costs.

Student Development
Assessment Techniques

Robert A. Mines

The student development practitioner has been challenged to use developmental theories for programming since the early to mid-1970s. In addition to applying developmental models in programming, the student development practitioner is also faced with issues of accountability and the call to use sophisticated evaluation techniques (Mines, Gressard, and Daniels, 1982). To meet these demands, the practitioner must turn to student development assessment techniques. This chapter reviews the existing techniques, introduces the practitioner to special issues related to developmental assessment, and outlines the next phase of instrument development needed in the field. This chapter assumes a pragmatic/utilitarian perspective on the use of assessment techniques. Within the framework of pragmatism and direct service utility, the existing instruments are evaluated by more stringent standards than are necessary for research purposes alone. The techniques not only need to be reliable and valid, they must be easy to administer, score, and interpret, or else they will not be of much help to the people who must conduct the administrative and program evaluations.

Developmental Assessment Issues

The assessment of developmental phenomena poses additional problems beyond those encountered within the traditional state-trait,

G. R. Hanson (Ed.). *Measuring Student Development.* New Directions
for Student Services, no. 20. San Francisco: Jossey-Bass, December 1982.

achievment testing, or behavioral assessment perspectives. Kitchener (see her chapter in the present volume) suggests that the length of time for cognitive stage change or task resolution almost precludes that a single student services level one program (Wirtz and Magrath, 1979) would have a significant impact on a selected developmental domain. Development does not end with graduation from college, so we are only measuring a specific segment of the developmental process. The data in the area of social-cognitive development support the assumption that stages are complex, not simple (see, for example, Mines, 1980; Rest, 1976). Any individual may manifest various stage levels in a given context and across content areas (that is, developmental decalage). Furthermore, the assumption that individuals progress through stages but do not regress is not supported. The attainment or resolution of developmental tasks is a complex phenomenon consisting of cognitive attitudinal and reasoning process changes as well as behavioral changes (for example, Chickering's vector of freeing of interpersonal relationships as discussed in Mines, 1978). Assessing developmental task resolution requires a complex multilevel approach.

In summary, the assessment of developmental stage change or task resolution presents general problems, such as the slowness of developmental change, the complex stage phenomenon, the issue of decalage (that is, stage change in one content area but not in another) and the assessment of cognitive and behavioral interaction for developmental task resolution. Test format and scoring variations also contribute to problems in assessing developmental change.

Assessment Formats for Measuring Development

Developmental researchers and student services practitioners are faced with several psychometric dilemmas. Are we trying to assess a developmental process (that is, a social-cognitive stage), or are we trying to "capture a developmental moment" as a landmark or sign of a given individual's development? Any time we try to reduce a process phenomenon to a static description we will introduce measurement error into our assessment.

The methodology format determines the type of information we will obtain. Rest (1976) distinguishes between preference, comprehension, and spontaneous use (production) of stage responses. An individual will prefer a higher stage response than he or she can comprehend or produce. It follows that one can comprehend a higher stage response than one can produce. The most conservative and taxing measure of stage level(s) is to have the individual produce his or her stage process in responding to the test items. Various formats have been used that elicit preference (Likert-type scales), comprehension (asking subjects to paraphrase or match statements), or production (open-ended or structured interviews). Rest (1976) states that "different tasks — manifest the acquisition of new ideas at different points of consolidation" (p. 202). The variety of formats eliciting different levels of stage acquisition limits the meaningfulness of inferences that can be made about stage level without a consideration of the task employed.

Production Formats. Open-ended or semistructured interview or sentence completion formats require students to produce a "stage typical" response. These formats assume that students cannot produce a response higher than their stage level. The students can produce lower stage responses. Typically, these assessment data are rated by two or more raters to produce a stage score.

There are two major advantages of this technique. It provides an open-ended data source for the refinement of the theory. It can be rated reliably (see, for example, Loevinger, 1976; Mines, 1981; Rest, 1976). The production format has its primary utility in basic developmental research. It is time consuming in terms of interviewer and/or rater time. It can also be costly to learn to rate the data or have the data rated (such as the Reflective Judgment Interview, Mines, 1980). This type of assessment format is neither practical nor efficient for most student services programming evaluation.

Preference and Comprehension Formats. Preference or comprehension formats are usually presented in a Likert-type scale or a multiple choice format. This type of format is used when the theory and stage typic responses have been identified and the purpose of the assessment is to "systematically inventory a subject's reactions to a standardized set of stimuli statements" (Rest, 1976, p. 201). In other words, when the purpose is to classify a person's stage level, a preference or comprehension test is preferable.

The advantage of this type of format is that it uses a consistent set of stage typical statements that minimizes the problem of having a subject wander or an interviewer using his or her clinical judgment to pursue ambiguous responses. The objective format does not allow any determination of the underlying developmental process used to arrive at a decision. The type of format used for a given developmental assessment technique affects the stage classification of a student.

Scoring Methods

Another area of controversy in developmental assessment that has a direct impact on stage classfication is the scoring method. There are a variety of scoring schemes in use. These vary from using the highest scored stage, the model level of stage usage (Loevinger, 1976), the percentage of highest stage exhibited (Rest, 1976), the predominant stage plus the second most used stage — which is then averaged by stage and across raters (Mines, 1981) — the use of cutting scores that use cumulative distributions of stage typical responses (Loevinger, 1976), or using a strong scalogram analysis that presents tasks that are stage typic in and of themselves (Fischer, Hand, and Russell, forthcoming).

Each of these methods has its liabilities, and only a few have any compelling merit beyond their initial heuristic value. The use of the highest stage score assumes that the student is motivated to produce his or her highest stage responses, which is not always the case (Mines, 1980). A major problem with the use of the highest stage is the assumption of a simple stage model. None of the major theorists (Fischer, Hand, and Russell, forthcoming; Loevinger, 1976; Rest, 1976) assumes a simple stage model. Furthermore, they argue that development is uneven and varies across content domains, so that using a single stage score does not represent the complexity of the phenomenon. The use of the modal stage response has the same simple stage assumption problems. The modal stage response underestimates the highest stage production or comprehension level of the subject. The implementation of the percentage of highest stage level produced is a positive move toward capturing the complexity of stage properties. The sole use of the highest stage percentage ignores the percentage of lower stage responses exhibited. The use of multiple stages in determining a score is used, for example, in reflective judgment scoring rules (see King, 1977). However, the complexity of the stage level is then diluted by averaging the stage levels across two raters (Mines, 1981). This results in a conservative estimate of stage functioning that is also affected by subject motivation and decalage problems across the test items. Loevinger (1976) addresses the complex stage scoring problem by using ogive rules of cumulative distributions. The use of these cutting scores is an important refinement in assessing developmental stages. Unfortunately, without a breakdown of stage typical responses, it is still difficult for the practitioner to use ogive rules in any sophisticated manner, because he or she is still left with a stage score that does not convey the intricacy or the interplay of the different stage skills.

Fischer, Hand, and Russell (forthcoming) have offered a variety of innovative scoring procedures in the cognitive development domain that may have potential in other social-cognitive areas as well as in developmental task models. Fischer and his colleagues have suggested that a strong scalogram could be used. This procedure predicts a sequence of steps in the acquisition of a developmental skill. A separate task is designed to assess each step. Each student's performance should then fit a Guttman Scale. This method eliminates the scoring algorithm problems discussed previously. It also eliminates the problem of using one developmental task to differentiate all of a model's developmental stages. "When every developmental stage is assessed independently, the assumption (the use of a single developmental task) is no longer a problem since it becomes a hypothesis to be tested" (Fischer, Hand, and Russell, forthcoming, p. 25). To date, such an approach to student development assessment does not exist in a format that would be useful to student services practitioners. Fischer and his colleagues present two other techniques/scoring methods that hold promise and are discussed in the recommendations for instrument development section of this chapter.

Student Development Assessment Techniques

Test format and scoring method issues have been briefly discussed to provide a conceptual framework for evaluating current student development assessment techniques. Due to limited space, selected theoretical domains and techniques are reviewed. The areas and instruments reviewed are: intellectual development (the Measurement of Intellectual Development [MID], the Reflective Judgment Interview), moral development (the Defining Issues Test), ego development (Loevinger and Wessler's Sentence Completion Test), and developmental task models (that is, Chickering's Vectors, the Student Development Task Inventory, and the "Iowa Instruments").

The Measurement of Intellectual Development (MID)

King (1978) notes that over eight different assessment methods have been used to determine the cognitive development position scores corresponding to Perry's (1970) theory of intellectual and ethical development. While the original interview methodology continues to be used to replicate and extend Perry's work (Clinchy, 1981; Mentkowski, 1981), it is time consuming and expensive, especially for applied situations. The major work in developing a practical alternative instrument was initiated by Knefelkamp (1974) and Widick (1975), who developed a paper-and-pencil measure that could be used both for research purposes and for feedback to faculty about how their students made meaning in the classroom. The instrument they created is called the Measure of Intellectual Development and, as the title implies, it focuses on the intellectual assets of the Perry model (positions 1–5).

Purpose and Nature of the Instrument. The MID is a semi-structured generation/production instrument designed to assess cognitive stage level in three specific domains: decision making, careers, and classroom learning. Each domain takes approximately fifteen minutes to complete. The MID essays are rated independently by two trained raters who then confer to reach a consensus rating. Each essay is given a three-digit rating that allows for an "elongation" of the Perry scheme (Knefelkamp, 1974). This scoring system provides stable position ratings as well as two transitional steps between each stable position. Standardized normative data are not available currently, although the instrument has been used with a variety of tradional-aged and nontraditional-aged, as well as graduate, students at numerous institutions throughout the country. The general cross-sectional results indicate freshmen to be largely in transition between positions 2 and 3, while juniors and seniors are in transition between positions 3 and 4 and in stable position 4. Sex differences have not been found. However, the authors point out that the instrument is *not* appropriate for international students, as cross-cultural differences (especially language) are likely to produce significant confounding effects.

Reliability. The MID is more reliably scored than most instruments assessing complex phenomena. The reliability studies conducted to date fall into one of three categories: correlations with interview ratings, correlations with external experts, and interrater reliability data of various kinds (see Table 1).

Clearly, the absolute agreement criterion is the most stringent, but, considering the complexity of assessing the degree to which a given subdominant position is reflected in transitional essays, the authors of the MID consider the dominant position agreement the most reasonable measure of interrater reliability.

Validity. A variety of approaches have been taken in addressing the issue of validity for the MID. Table 2 shows correlations representing convergent/divergent validity data between the MID and other construct and developmental models. The MID correlates moderately well with conceptual level (.51), with the Defining Issues Test (DIT) in one study (.45, Meyer, 1977), but not in another (.13, Wertheimer, 1980), and with a measure of ego development (.30) by Wertheimer (1980). The correlations shown in Table 2 suggest that, while there is some overlap among the various developmental dimensions, they seem to be reasonably distinct domains. The relationships with empathy and locus of control are consistent with the implications of the Perry (1970) scheme and provide additional evidence to suggest the validity of the MID.

Table 1. Measure of Intellectual Development—Reliability Data

	Mentkowski (1981)	Moore (1982)	Slepitza (1976)	Wertheimer (1976)	Widick (1975)	Stephenson, Hunt (1977)	Allen (1982)	Meyer (1977)
Correlations with interview ratings	NA*	NA	.74	77	NA	NA	NA	NA
Correlations with expert raters	.45[1] .76[2]	NA	NA	NA	NA	NA .73 – .87[2]	.42 – .64[1]	NA
Interrater agreement	.43[1] .74[2]	.58[1] .83[2]	.93	.93	.35 – .62[1] .87 – 1.00[2]	.82	NA	.91 – .93

*NA: Not Applicable
[1] Absolute agreement
[2] Dominant position agreement

Table 2. Validity Data: Comparisons Between MID Ratings and Various Constructs/Models

	Widick (1975)	Wertheimer (1980)	Allgire (1977)	Meyer (1977)	Mason (1978)	Viesar (1978)	Bogar (1981)
Ego Development (Loevinger)	NA*	.30	NA	NA	NA	NA	NA
Moral Development (Kohlberg, DIT)	NA	.13	NA	.45	NA	NA	NA
Conceptual Level (Schroder, Driver, and Streufert, 1967)	.51	NA	NA	NA	NA	NA	NA
Empathy	NA	NA	NA	NA	.14, .32	.13	.31[1]
Locus of Control	NA	NA	NA	NA	−.19, −.54	NA	NA
Information Responsiveness[2]	NA	NA	.42	NA	NA	NA	NA

NA*: Not Applicable
[1] Attitudes Towards Women Scales (AWS)
[2] measured by the WAIS

Face validity, criterion group differences, and experimental enhancement studies are other methods of establishing the validity of the MID. The MID's particular focus on classroom learning and student-generated open-ended responses lends critical face validity to the instrument. Cross-sectional and short-term longitudinal studies summarized by Moore (1982) reflect expected freshman–senior differences predicted by the Perry scheme. In several experimental studies, the MID has been used to examine differences in pre–post gains related to developmentally designed classroom experiences. The differential gains in the theoretically predicted direction add further credence to the instrument's relation to its underlying construct (see Table 3).

The major strength of the MID is that it has incorporated a standard structure in a written response format for a specific content domain during the theory development phase of the Perry (1970) research. It yields production type responses that are heuristically rich. It can be consistently scored by trained raters with an acceptable percentage of agreement. The MID can easily be administered in a group situation, which is a plus for the student services practitioner. The MID can be scored at the Center for Applications of Developmental Instruction for a reasonable fee ($3.00 per protocol). See the final chapter in this volume for the complete address. The MID has resolved one aspect of the decalage issue in adult intellectual development by focusing on specific content domains (that is, classroom, career). Student services practitioners should use the MID in programs designed to impact on these areas. The validity of using it in other areas is untested at this time. Further components could be developed for areas such as residence services, counseling centers, and so on.

The major liabilities of the MID are its scoring system and the time expense of learning to use the scoring system. The scoring system

Table 3. Experimental Enhancement Studies Using the MID

	Knefelkamp Widick (1975)	*Stephenson, Hunt (1977)*	*Touchton and others (1977)*	*Clement and others (1977)*
Average Stage Movement	.85[1], .79[2]	.85[3], .42[4], .12[4]	.59[3], .39[5], .17[4]	.54

[1]Dualist treatment
[2]Relativist treatment
[3]Experimental treatment
[4]Control group
[5]Quasi-experimental group

underestimates the level of complexity the individual is capable of understanding but is a reasonably accurate estimate of a person's ability to *produce* specific levels of cognitive complexity, as is often required in classroom settings. Users of the MID need to recognize that students may well be able to comprehend or express a preference for a higher level of cognitive complexity. The MID also does not differentiate among the domains of cognitive complexity, specific cognitive skills, epistemology, and metaphystical assumptions about reality. These domains appear to be separate yet interrelated in adult intellectual development (Kitchener and King, 1981). The scoring system does not represent the complexity of stage interaction that appears in early adulthood; rather, the rating criteria for the MID are based on narrowly defined, specific content domains that assume a single stage model within each domain.

The next steps in the continuing development of the MID will examine the relationship between the MID ratings of Perry (1970) position and critical thinking or writing skills. What, for example, are the necessary concomitant skills for true contextually relativistic reasoning? Additional work on the rating and scoring system is planned to clarify the distinctions between stage/position cues and style/topology cues. Also, more work is planned to collect normative data from nontraditional learners — that is, older students and noncollege groups.

Reflective Judgment Interview (RJI)

The reflective judgment model of young adult intellectual development has a great deal of promise. It is partially based on Perry's (1970) model but does not have the conceptual confounding with intellectual and identity concerns that Perry's model has. Over ten dissertations and research projects have been completed to date using the reflective judgment interview (RJI). (See, for example, Brabeck, 1980; Kitchener and King, 1981; Mines, 1980; Strange, 1978; Welfel, 1979; and Wood, 1980).

Purpose and Nature of the Instrument. The RJI is copyrighted by Karen Kitchener and Patricia King. Information regarding it can be obtained from Kitchener at GCB 112, School of Education, University of Denver, Denver, CO 80208. The RJI is a semistructured interview and elicits production-type data to provide a description of the subject's intellectual stage functioning. The interview is administered individually and takes about one hour to complete. During the interview, one of four dilemmas (the dilemmas are of a social issue nature and can be found in King, 1977) are presented verbally while the subject follows along on an identical written copy. After each dilemma is read, the interviewer asks a series of standard probe questions. The subject's responses are tape recorded separately. All of the tape recordings (that is, four per subject) are transcribed and rated blind by certified raters.

Kitchener and King require that anyone using the RJI use certified interviewers and raters or become certified themselves in order to assure comparability of results across the studies. At this time, there is no charge for the certification process other than mailing and phone expenses. Certified raters have charged from $7.00 to $25.00 per subject to rate the RJI. The major expenses of the RJI are the costs of audio tapes, recording equipment, transcription of tapes, duplicating costs, and time.

The RJI assumes that reflective judgment stages are complex, as opposed to simple stages. This assumption is not realized in the current scoring rules. The current scoring rules require the raters to include a major stage response and a second major stage response for each dilemma that are then averaged across dilemmas and across raters, resulting in a single stage score. In a critique of this psychometrically conservative treatment of the RJI raw scores, Mines (1980) notes that the interview responses are more complex than the averaging of the dilemma scores indicates.

The RJI has been developed on traditional-age high school, college, and graduate student populations and on two noncollege populations (see Lawson, 1980; Shoff, 1979). Normative data in and of itself has not been compiled, although Welfel (1981) has reviewed the data in a study-by-study format. The majority of the research has been done at large state universities (for example, the University of Minnesota, the University of Iowa, the University of Utah), with the exception of Brabeck's (1980) study on a small liberal arts campus.

Reliability. As an interview procedure requiring the use of two raters, the RJI and rating rules are more reliably scored with a high interrater agreement than most techniques that assess complex processes. The RJI has moderate to high internal consistency as determined by the dilemma total correlations. (See Table 4.) The Cronbach alpha estimate of reliability indicates the interrelationship among a set of items comprising a scale. The higher the value, the more likely that the items are measuring the same construct. Measures of equivalence or internal consistency are high using Cronbach's alpha. (See Table 5.) The Interjudge reliability of the RJI has ranged from a high of .96 (King, 1977) to moderate .53 to .63 (Strange, 1978). (See Table 6.) Finally, the interrater agreement scores of the RJI are moderately high for the first round of rating. (See Table 7.)

Table 4. Dilemma–Total Correlations

Dilemma	King (1977)	Strange (1978)	Shoff (1979)	Mines (1980)	Brabeck (1980)
1	.90	.67, .78, .45	.62	.71	.77
2	.89	.66, .55, .48	.83	.75	.76
3	.91	.57, .62, .38	.74	.81	.73
4	.92	.78, .42, .58	.84	.75	.78

Validity. The validity of the RJI is intertwined with the validity of the reflective judgment model. To validate a developmental model, cross-sectional and longitudinal data are needed as well as convergent and divergent validity data. The majority of the research on the construct and the instrument has been cross-sectional (Kitchener, 1981). These studies support the age and education trends in the theoretically predicted direction. One longitudinal study has been completed (King and others, 1982). Stage change was in the appropriate direction. The convergent and divergent validity studies have focused on four major competing constructs: formal operations, verbal ability, general academic aptitude, and critical thinking skills (Brabeck, 1981). In Brabeck's (1981) review, she notes that formal operations (King, 1977), verbal reasoning (Kitchener, 1977), general academic ability (see Brabeck, 1980; Mines, 1980; Welfel, 1979), and critical thinking skills (Brabeck, 1980; Mines, 1980) do not account for differences in reflective judgment scores and probably represent a necessary but not sufficient relationship to advanced intellectual development. This advanced intellectual development could be due to a combination of additional cognitive skills development (Mines, 1980) and changes in epistemological assumptions across stage levels (Brabeck, 1980; Kitchener, 1981).

Summary and Evaluation. The RJI generates theoretically rich data that has strong heuristic value for continued research on intellectual development. The RJI is sound psychometrically and has adequate reliability and good interrater agreement. The implementation of a certification process for raters and interviewers ensures that variations in ratings across studies are more likely to be due to actual affects than to

Table 5. Internal Consistency

Overall Cronbach's alpha	King (1977)	Strange (1978)	Shoff (1979)	Mines (1980)	Brabeck (1980)
	.96	.63 to .85	not rep.	.71	.77

Table 6. Overall Interjudge Reliability

King (1977)	Strange (1978)	Shoff (1979)	Mines (1980)	Brabeck (1980)
.96	.53 to .63	.51	.83	.90

rating or interviewing error. This will enhance the comparability of the studies, thus minimizing problems that have existed, for example, in the Perry (1970) research.

The RJI is expensive in terms of training, time of administration, transcription time and costs, and time and cost of rating. It is more appropriate for student services research than for program evaluation. The interview format is semistructured and allows for the stimulus to be presented to the subject in various ways. However, the responses may be due to factors other than differences in stage level. Brabeck (1980) and Mines (1980) have both suggested that ambiguities exist in the rating rules at the middle and upper ends of the model. Brabeck (1980) notes that the individual dilemmas of the RJI warrant further examination of their measurement characteristics, as they have a low to moderate intercorrelation.

The next step in RJI development and refinement involves the resolution of conceptual as well as measurement issues. The major conceptual issue involves the concept of stage and the representation of the stage(s) in the scoring scheme. The current scoring system needs to be revised, as it underestimates the highest stage of production by the subject and also reduces the complexity of the response to a single stage score through the averaging of the dilemma scores. The scoring rules need to reflect the complexity of the model and of the optimal stage usage of the subject.

The unit of analysis in the rating of the RJI also needs to be clearly defined. It is not clear whether each thought, each sentence, each paragraph, or the total transcript constitutes the phenomenon that is rated. As the rating procedure currently exists, raters have focused on all of the above in varying degrees and then come up with a rating for the dilemma. Given this variability, it is a credit to the scoring rules that the interrater agreement is as high as it is.

Table 7. First Round Interrater Agreement

King (1977)	Strange (1978)	Shoff (1979)	Mines (1980)	Brabeck (1980)
.77	.70, .76, .64	.74	.71	.76

Currently an objective reflective judgment test does not exist. However, two groups of researchers, Schmidt and Davis at the University of Minnesota and Strange and King, Bowling Green State, are independently developing objective format reflective judgment tests. The development of an objective format is necessary to provide a practical intellectual development assessment technique that the student services practitioner can use in program evaluation.

The development of an objective instrument needs to answer the question: Is the test going to have a preference, comprehension, or production format? The answer to this question has a direct bearing on the construction of items and the stage property inferences that can be made.

The issue of recognition versus production tests was played out in the moral reasoning research between Kohlberg's (1971) interview and Rest's (1976) Defining Issues Tests. Rest (1976) concluded that the recognition test is measuring something other than Kohlberg's model of moral reasoning. It remains to be seen whether the assessment techniques of the reflective judgment model will follow a similar metamorphosis.

Finally, the existing RJI data needs to be reanalyzed to further our understanding of the psychometric properties of the existing instrument. Brabeck (1980) has suggested that the psychometric properties of the individual dilemmas be investigated further, as it appears that they may be eliciting various stage level responses. She has also called for the investigation of alternative scoring methods.

The RJI has been invaluable as an exploratory instrument. As Kitchener notes in her chapter in the present volume, what is needed in assessing developmental change is not a global or epochal assessment but a finer-grained assessment. The next step in intellectual developmental stage assessment is to look at specific cognitive skills that are part of a given stage (Fischer, Hand, and Russell, forthcoming; Mines, 1980) and to develop instruments that can assess epistemological perspectives.

Moral Development

The Defining Issues Test (DIT)

The DIT is designed to assess moral development from a cognitive stage perspective. The DIT has one of the more substantial data bases of the current developmental assessment techniques. Rest (1979) has an ongoing instrument refinement project at the University of Minnesota. He requests in the DIT manual that individuals who use the DIT send him copies of the data to be added to the data file.

Purpose and Nature of the Instrument. The DIT is a recognition test rather than a production test. It therefore produces higher stage levels than an interview or sentence completion format. The DIT consists of a long form (six stories) and a short form (three stories). The DIT contains an instruction page and three or six stories that reflect various moral dilemmas. The subject is asked to mark his or answers directly on the test, although machine scorable answer sheets can be developed

The DIT can be administered to students in ninth grade or above. The long form can be administered in a large group setting, and fifty minutes is usually sufficient for completing it, with most people completing it in thirty to forty minutes. The short form takes fifteen to thirty minutes to complete. The DIT is an objectively scored instrument and can be hand scored by clerical help or by a computer-scoring program provided by Rest (1979). If these two options are not feasible, a scoring service is offered by the Minnesota Moral Research Project that is relatively inexpensive (contact Rest for current prices).

The scoring systems provide a profile of the percentage of each stage level marked by the subject, plus the P score, which is the percentages of principled responses, an empirical weighted scored called the D score, A scores, which are an antiestablishment rating, a reliability check called the M score, and a consistency check. The P score and the D are the most often used for research purposes. Rest (1979) also recommends use of a stage profile approach. A positive feature of the DIT is its use of the M score to identify subjects who mark items on the basis of the "pretentiousness rather than the meaning" (Rest, 1979, p. 52). The consistency check is a monitor on the usability of the subject's responses. This gives an indication of the seriousness with which the subject approached the test.

Reliability. The DIT manual (Rest, 1979) reports test-retest reliabilities across several studies as generally in the high .70s or .80s and Cronbach's alpha internal consistency indices in the high .70s. The reliabilities for the specific stage scores are more moderate in the .50s and .60s. Rest strongly suggests that caution needs to be used in interpreting stage scores because of lower reliabilities. As the DIT is an objective instrument with objective scoring methods, interjudge agreement, reliability, or interviewer consistency are not of concern. Alternative forms of the DIT do not exist yet.

Validity. The DIT appears to have adequate criterion validity. Rest (1979) reports that, in six studies, significant differences in scores have been found across age and education levels in the theoretically predicted direction. Several longitudinal studies have been completed that report significant upward stage changes over four and six years. Furthermore, this upward stage movement cannot be accounted for by generational or cohort specific effects. The convergent-divergent validity data indicates correlations up to the .60s and .70s with Kohlberg's (1971) various test versions. The DIT has correlations of .20 to .50 with measures of cognitive development and intelligence (Rest, 1979). It is usually nonsignificant or inconsistent with personality, and attitude measures as well as demographic variables such as sex, socioeconomic class, and political party.

Rest (1979) also provides some unique validation data not available on most of the developmental instruments. In a review of sixteen experimental enhancement studies, none of the control groups and only two of the experimental groups showed any gains in moral development. In all cases, the movement shown was less than in the longitudinal studies (Rest, 1979). This suggests that the DIT is measuring underlying conceptual organization and not just a specialized content. A second approach was to have subjects "fake good" and "fake bad." Subjects were able to "fake bad" and lower their scores but were not able to increase their scores by "faking good." The last approach reviewed implementing scaled techniques. Rest (1979) reports a study by Davison, Robbins, and Swanson (1978) in which the average scale values of items, when grouped according to their theoretical stage, were in the predicted order. Stage two had the lowest value, stage three the next, and so on up the model.

Summary and Evaluation. Rest (1979) provides an impressive array of data on the reliability and validity of the DIT. The extent and variety of studies on the DIT suggest that the DIT is a solid measure of moral reasoning. The ease of administering and scoring makes the DIT an attractive instrument for student services practitioners who are interested in this aspect of cognitive development. As with all of the cognitive stage models, change is slow and single programs probably will not affect stage change as measured by the DIT. The DIT provides a comprehensive scoring procedure that reflects the complexity of the stages. The major limitation of the DIT (which is true for all the cognitive stage instruments) is the inability to measure the fine-grained aspects of the stages, such as stage specific cognitive skill change or epistemological and metaphysical changes related to moral reasoning. The development of assessment techniques that reflect these stage specific changes will be of greater utility for evaluating social-cognitive stage change.

Ego Development

Sentence Completion Test

The Sentence Completion Test (SC) is used to assess ego development level as described by Loevinger's (1976) model. This is the third area of social-cognitive stage assessment that will be reviewed. Other models, such as Marcia's (1966), may also be of value to student services practitioners but are not reviewed here due to space limitations.

Purpose and Nature of the Instrument. Loevinger and Wessler (1970) describe ego development as the master trait. All other forms of development, such as intellectual, moral, the self-system, interpersonal relationships, character development, and others are subsumed under the concept of ego development. One of the basic assumptions of the SC is that there are "coherent meanings in experience. . . . [This] is the essence of the ego or ego functioning, rather than one among many equally important ego functions. The ego maintains its stability, its identity, and its coherence by selectively gating out observations inconsistent with its current state. (One man's coherence, however, is another man's gibberish" (Loevinger and Wessler, 1970, p. 8).

The SC is a production test that attempts to identify qualitative differences in ego level. The SC consists of thirty-six incomplete sentence stems. The subject is asked to complete the sentences in any way he or she wants and takes fifteen to thirty minutes to complete the test. A number of different forms for girls, women, boys, and men are available in Loevinger and Wessler (1970). Thus the cost is minimal, involving institutional reproduction costs. The scoring of the SC requires two trained raters. Loevinger and Wessler (1970) provide a self-training guide, or one can be trained at Washington University in St. Louis. The SC can be administered in large groups. The age range is from eleven through adulthood. The original test development samples were all female. A scoring manual for males has not been published yet. Loevinger and Wessler (1970) suggest adapting the rules for females until the manual for males is published. The basic scoring system uses ogive rules or cutting points for determining stage level. The ogive rules take stage complexity into account but end up assigning a single stage score to the subject.

Norms. The original sample was a cross-section of females ranging in age from eleven to fifty-plus, from a variety of races, marital statuses, and educational and socioeconomic statuses. The norms for males have not been published. Subgroup norms are not available.

Reliability. Loevinger and Wessler report interrater agreement by pairs of raters that range from 60–86, 63–91, and 65–94 percent across three pairs of raters. The medians for the percentage agreement across the rater pairs were 77, 78, and 81. The interrater correlations for the three rater pairs were .49-.88, .53-.93, and .56-.96. The median reliabilities were .75, .76, and .76, respectively. It is important to note that these reliabilities and agreements were obtained between raters that had little or no background in psychology. The correlations of four self-trained raters with a composite-trained rater were .60-.89, .57-.98, and .44-.89 across the thirty-six items. The median correlations were .78, .79, .85, and .76. The Cronbach alpha coefficients were .91 for a composite-trained rater over 543 subjects and .92, .90, and .88 for the composite-trained rater and two self-trained raters on a subsample of 100 subjects.

Loevinger and Wessler (1970) report extensive information on the reliability and percent agreement of raters on the total protocol ratings. The percent agreements across two samples were .50-.72, and .53-.80 with medians of .61 and .72 for ten pairs of raters. The percent agreements within half a stage level were 88–97 and 91–100, with a median of 94 for both samples. The interrater correlations ranged from .78 to .93, with a median of .85. A final indice of overall rater reliability is the correlations of trained and self-trained raters with the criterion total protocol rating and with the composite rater ogive score. The correlations across five trained raters for the criterion total protocol rating ranged from .90 to .96, and for the composite rater ogive score the range was .86 and .92, with the criterion total protocol rating .83 and .93 with the composite rater ogive score.

The SC has a high degree of interrater reliability and agreement. The internal consistency of the SC is high, although the alphas across subsamples were not reported. These alphas would be expected to be lower. One of the outstanding aspects of Loevinger and Wessler's (1970) interrater agreement and reliability data is the performance of the self-trained raters. This reflects the extent to which the authors have gone in refining the scoring manual and the advantage of objective criteria for assigning levels to a protocol.

Validity. The validation of a developmental stage measure is a multifaceted, ongoing endeavor, as has been noted. The SC appears to measure a unitary dimension structure. Factor analysis results indicate that the first factor correlates at .999 and with the sum of the item ratings (Loevinger and Wessler, 1970).

The construct validity information indicates that the SC total protocol ratings correlate .58 and .61 with an open-ended interview. Initial cross-sectional studies suggest progressive age differences across the ego levels. The SC score correlates .45 with IQ scores for black sixth grade boys and .47 for the girls.

Summary and Evaluation. The SC has good interrater reliability and internal consistency. The initial cross-sectional validity data are promising. For the student services practitioner, the SC is easy to obtain and administer. The low cost of the SC makes it attractive. It is somewhat time consuming to learn to rate the SC.

The major drawback in using the SC comes not from the instrument but from the nature of the developmental phenomena it assesses. Change in ego development is a slow process. In one study, a full stage change had not occurred in one year (King, Mines, and Barratt, 1979). Thus the construct may not be too useful for student services programming purposes.

The scoring rules for the SC are an important improvement over the use of the mode, mean, or highest stage approaches. Ogive rules do not represent the stage complexity that probably exists in ego development. Refining this aspect of the rules will be an important advancement.

Loevinger (1976) calls ego development the master trait, but all of the threads of ego development do not represent the whole. It will be important for the student services practitioner to separate out some of the threads in order to do any program planning with this model and to develop specific assessment techniques for those subsets of ego development.

Developmental Task Models

Developmental task models represent another approach to the conceptualization of adult development. Developmental tasks are culturally specific events that occur at approximately the same time in the life of a given age cohort. A task must be successfully resolved for a person to develop the experiential foundation to resolve later developmental tasks, although, to date, there is little or no evidence of a longitudinal nature to support this assumption.

Developmental task models present a complex measurement picture. The models present a specific goal that young adults must attain (for example, freeing interpersonal relationships). The attainment of this goal requires multilevel changes. For example, in Chickering's (1969) vector of freeing of interpersonal relationships in order to move from dependence to independence to interdependence as well as increasing one's tolerance for diversity, it is reasonable to assume the individual must experience a shift in cognitive complexity. Cognitive complexity as viewed by Perry (1970) or Kitchener and King (1981) is necessary if we are to move from banal stereotypic views of others to a sophisticated appreciation for individuals from diverse backgrounds. Cognitive stage change is implied in being able to process the interrelations by assessing the compromises and benefits necessary to relate interdependently. Also implicit in the resolution of this task are changes in ego and moral development levels. Ego development changes are necessary for the self-awareness necessary to act interdependently. Moral development changes reflect the implicit social contracts of dependent relationships versus interdependent relationships. The assessment of cognitive stage change and/or attitudinal change is one aspect of assessing a developmental task.

Developmental tasks can also be considered from a skills perspective. Each task has certain skills that the individual must possess in order to resolve the task. For example, the freeing of an interpersonal relationships vector requires that the individual possess certain communications skills to be able to function interdependently. Assertiveness skills, conflict mediation skills, and basic communications skills, such as those mentioned by Egan (1982), are skill categories that would be helpful in living interdependently. However, we do not have any data regarding specific skills required for task resolution. As with the cognitive stage assessment problems, the identification and assessment of task-related skills may provide us with a more refined understanding of the components of developmental task resolution.

The third aspect of the developmental tasks is behavior. Perhaps we should assess the behaviors related to task resolution. The assumption is that if one exhibits task-related behavior, one has resolved the task. This perspective has some appeal, in that it eliminates the problems of assessing cognitive stage, skills, and attitudes and goes directly to the behavioral manifestations. This approach is probably sufficient if the behaviors can be identified and one is only concerned with a yes or no diagnosis of task resolution. Unfortunately, the resolution of a developmental task is a process, not an event. The process occurs over time and, as noted previously, involves cognitive and skill changes as well as behavioral changes. Assessing only behavior tells the student services practitioner nothing about the why of an individual's progress in task resolution or programming needs. Behavioral assessment does not provide us with any clues as to how or even where to intervene. The limits of using a behavioral assessment approach to task resolution must be kept in mind.

The best approach to developmental task assessment would

integrate the cognitive stage, skills, and behavioral dimensions. The second best alternative would be to identify specific skills related to task resolution as well as behavioral manifestations of the task. The least desirable approach would be to assess only one dimension or even one aspect of the dimensions. We do not have the research base at this time to know what the relationship of cognitive complexity or attitudinal changes is to behavioral indicators of task resolution. In a related area, moral development research indicates that moral stage level is not a very good predictor of behavior (Rest, 1976).

There has been relatively little developmental task instrument development. Chickering's (1969) vectors of young adult development had received consistent attention from student services practitioners and researchers. This section will review the instrumentation designed to assess Chickering's vectors.

Chickering's model consists of seven vectors on developmental tasks that college age young adults need to resolve. The seven vectors are: achieving competence, managing emotions, becoming autonomous, establishing identity, freeing interpersonal relationships, clarifying purposes, and developing integrity. (See Chickering, 1969, for a complete description). The major instrument development (which focuses on behavioral aspects) has been done by Winston, Miller, and Prince (1979) at the University of Georgia. A second group of instruments focusing on attitudinal aspects of freeing of interpersonal relationships, clarifying purpose, and establishing identity were developed at the University of Iowa by Mines (1978), Barratt (1978), and Erwin and Delworth (1978), respectively. These instruments are still preliminary, although cross-sectional and convergent validity data (Rodgers, 1982) and four-year longitudinal change data (Hood, 1982) have been reported on the Iowa instruments. As the Iowa instruments are in the early instrument development phases, they will not be reviewed in this chapter. The Student Development Task Inventory-2 (Winston, Miller, and Prince, 1979) is reviewed in the next section, as it has received the most development to date.

Student Development Task Inventory-2 (SDTI-2)

Purpose and Nature of the Instrument. The SDTI-2 "represents a sample of behaviors which students can be expected to demonstrate when they have satisfactorily achieved certain developmental tasks" (Winston, Miller, and Prince, 1979, p. 6). The SDTI-2 consists of three scales that assess the developmental tasks of developing autonomy, developing purpose, and freeing of interpersonal relationships. The three major task areas are each divided into three subtasks. The SDTI-2 consists of 140 items that are marked true or false. It takes twenty to thirty minutes to complete. The answer sheet consists of two parts, an original and a carbon copy for the student. The SDTI-2 is designed to assess the development of individual college students from seventeen to twenty-three years old. It is intended to be used to assess behaviors related to task resolution or for stimulating discussion around personal growth issues. The SDTI-2 can be administered individually or in groups. The cost for a sample packet is $7.00. The answer sheets and booklets cost 35¢ and 75¢ each.

Norms. The authors specifically state that the SDTI-2 is to be used for individual students and there is no need to establish norms or to attempt interpretations by making references to the performances of groups of students. The SDTI-2 was developed in a systematic manner through four phases. The SDTI-2 was refined on a sample ($N = 497$) of college students at twenty colleges and universities across the country. The SDTI-2 samples have consisted of eighteen to twenty-two year old college students, of both sexes, white and black racial backgrounds, and freshman through senior class standing.

Reliability. The SDTI-2 manual reports test-retest and internal consistency reliability information. The two-week test-retest correlations for the total inventory were .90. The range of test-retest reliability coefficients for the scales was from .85 to .93, with the majority clustering around .90. The Cronbach's alpha internal consistency coefficients for the total inventory and scales were: total inventory, .90; developing autonomy, .78; developing purpose, .85; and developing mature interpersonal relationships, .73. The SDTI-2 subscales' alpha coefficients ranged from .45 to .78, with four of the nine having alphas at .51 or below. The subscale reliabilities are low, and they should be interpreted with great caution.

Validity. The SDTI-2 has constrasted group and concurrent validity data. Four contrasted groups were identified by residence hall staff members: active daters, nondaters, joiners, and social isolates. These groups were used to validate the subscales of the developing mature interpersonal relationships scale. Joiners and active daters scored higher on the scale score than did the nondaters and social isolates. The joiners also scored significantly higher than the social isolates on the mature relationships with peers subscale but not on the other two subscales. The active daters scored significantly higher than the nondaters on the intimate relationships with the opposite sex subscale but not on the other two subscales. Students who had not developed appropriate skills in relating to peers or were not dating were identified by the scales.

The concurrent validity studies correlated the Study Habits, Family Independence, and Peer Independence subscales of the College Student Questionnaire (CSQ) and the Adult Form I of the Career Development Inventory with SDTI-2. The Study Habits Scale correlated significantly but moderately with the Developing Autonomy scale, Instrumental Autonomy subscale, Developing Purpose scale, Appropriate Educational Plans subscale and the Nature Lifestyle Plans subscale. Family Independence correlated significantly but in the low moderate range with the Emotional Autonomy and Mature Career Plans subscales. Finally, the Peer Independence scale had a significant low moderate correlation with the Emotional Autonomy subscale. These correlations were all in the theoretically predicted direction, thus giving initial support to those SDTI-2 scales.

The Crystallization, Specification, and Implementation scales of the Career Development Inventory all had significant low moderate correlations with the Developing Purpose scale. The Implementation scale also correlated with the Developing Autonomy scale.

Significant age differences were only found on the Appropriate Educational Plans and the Mature Career Plans subscales. The only sex differences were found on the Developing Mature Interpersonal Relationships scale and the Tolerance subscale. Females scored higher than males on both scales. There were no differences between blacks and whites on any of the scales. The widest range of differences were found according to class standing. Significant differences were found on the Developing Autonomy and Developing Purpose scales as well as the Instrumental Autonomy, Interdependence, Appropriate Educational Plans, and Mature Career Plans subscales. The authors suggest these findings highlight the impact the college environment has upon an individual's development.

Summary and Evaluation. The SDTI-2 is one of the first major instrument development efforts designed to assess young adult task development. It approaches the assessment problem by focusing on behaviors that should be task related. The instrument has good internal consistency, and the initial validity studies are promising.

The question of how to assess developmental tasks becomes central in evaluating the SDTI-2. As noted earlier, the attainment of a developmental task involves cognitive complexity and attitudinal as well as behavioral changes. The SDTI-2 only uses behavioral indicators; thus we lose a significant aspect of the developmental change. The second area that needs further refinement is the scale development. The authors discuss scale and subscale differences, yet the scales and subscales are not orthogonal. This raises the question of how well the SDTI-2 discriminates among the various groups. At this point only the scales should be used to make inferences. The scoring system is one of the major liabilities of the SDTI-2. The behaviors are summed to give a scale score. This would be fine if the scales were Guttman-type scales; however, they are not. The scales are treated like modified Likert-type scales. The reason this distinction is important is that statistically significant differences may be found but the differences may not be developmentally significant. For example, class standing differences were found on the Developing Purpose scale with the means as follows: freshmen, 27.92; sophomores, 29.91; juniors, 31.07; and seniors, 34.03. If these were Guttman scales, we would be able to infer which behaviors the upperclassmen had mastered that the underclassmen had not. As the scoring system now exists, we cannot infer anything other than that upperclassmen report more developmentally appropriate behaviors. We do not know at this point whether or not the task has been resolved. These three areas set the stage (so to speak) for the next phase of developmental task instrument development.

Conclusions and Future Directions

The current state of the art in young adult developmental stage and task assessment is not refined to the extent that student services practitioners can easily or meaningfully use the techniques. The field is posed on the brink of a new generation of assessment techniques. The areas for refinement and the specifics for refinement of the new generation of techniques are discussed in depth in Hanson's chapter. These techniques will have to incorporate complex stage scoring systems. Multilevel assessment for developmental tasks is necessary. Some of the more innovative assessment ideas have evolved from Fischer, Hand, and Russell's (forthcoming) work. They call for the implementation of strong scalogram analysis and the use of practice manipulations on developmental skills/tasks to determine maximum developmental performances. The new generation of instruments will incorporate specific skills related to a given stage as opposed to global descriptors. Finally, the new generation of instruments will be cost-effective and have utility for the student services practitioner who is faced with the challenge of developmental programming and evaluation.

References

Allen, K. Unpublished master's thesis, University of Maryland–College Park, 1982.

Allgire, N. E. "Developmental Instruction and Information Responsiveness: Their Effects on Cognitive Development and Empathy." Unpublished doctoral dissertation, University of Maryland, 1977.

Barratt, W. R. "Developing Purposes Inventory." *Technical Report.* Iowa City: College of Education, University of Iowa, 1978.

Bogar, C. "The Relationship Between Attitudes Toward Women and Cognitive Complexity in Undergraduate College Students." Unpublished thesis, University of Maryland–College Park, 1981.

Brabeck, M. "The Relationship Between Criticial Thinking Skills and the Development of Reflective Judgment." Unpublished doctoral dissertation, University of Cincinnati, 1980.

Chickering, A. W. *Education and Identity.* San Francisco: Jossey-Bass, 1969.

Clement, L., Agar, J., Sherman, M., and Sobol, J. "Paraprofessionals — Development of Our Systems and Our Human Resources: A Model for Training." Paper presented at the University of Maryland Student Affairs Conference, University of Maryland–College Park, March, 1977.

Clinchy, B. "A Longitudinal Study of the Cognitive Development of Women." Paper presented at the Perry Conference, St. Paul, Minnesota, June, 1981.

Davison, M. L., Robbins, S., and Swanson, D. "Stage Structure in Objective Moral Judgments." *Developmental Psychology,* 1978, *14,* 137–146.

Egan, G. *The Skilled Helper.* Monterey, Calif.: Brooks/Cole, 1982.

Erwin, T. D., and Delworth, U. "Erwin-Delworth Identity Scale." *Technical Report.* Iowa City: College of Education, University of Iowa, 1978.

Fischer, K. W., Hand, H. H., and Russell, S. L. "The Development of Abstractions in Adolescence and Adulthood." In M. Commons (Ed.), *Beyond Formal Operations.* New York: Praeger, forthcoming.

Hood, A. B. "Student Development on Three Vectors Over Four Years." Paper presented at the meeting of the American College Personnel Association National Convention, Detroit, Michigan, March, 1982.

King, P. M. "The Development of Reflective Judgment and Formal Operational Thinking in Adolescents and Young Adults." Unpublished doctoral dissertation, University of Minnesota, 1977.

King, P. M. "William Perry's Theory of Intellectual and Ethical Development." In L. Knefelkamp, C. Widick, and C. Parker (Eds.), *New Directions for Student Services: Applying New Developmental Findings,* no. 4. San Francisco: Jossey-Bass, 1978.

King, P. M., Mines, R. A., and Barratt, W. R. "Longitudinal Study of Developmental Changes During the Freshman Year." Paper presented at the American College Personnel Association National Convention, Los Angeles, March, 1979.

King, P. M., Kitchener, K. S., Davison, M. L., Parker, C., and Wood, P. K. "The Justification of Beliefs in Young Adults: A Longitudinal Study." Unpublished manuscript, School of Education, University of Denver, 1982.

Kitchener, K. S. "Intellectual Development in Late Adolescents and Young Adults: Reflective Judgment and Verbal Reasoning." Unpublished doctoral dissertation, University of Minnesota, 1977.

Kitchener, K. S. "Does Development Occur in Reflective Judgment in the Young Adult Years?" Paper presented at the meeting of the American College Personnel Association, Cincinnati, Ohio, April, 1981.

Kitchener, K. S., and King, P. M. "Reflective Judgment: Concepts of Justification and Their Relationship to Age and Education." *Journal of Applied Developmental Psychology,* 1981, *2,* 89–116.

Knefelkamp, L. "Developmental Instruction: Fostering Intellectual and Personal Growth in College Students." Unpublished doctoral dissertation, University of Minnesota, 1974.

Kohlberg, L. "Stages of Moral Development." In C. M. Beck, B. S. Crittenden, and E. V. Sullivan (Eds.), *Moral Education.* Toronto: University of Toronto Press, 1971.

Lawson, J. "The Relationship Between Graduate Education and the Development of Reflective Judgment: A Function of Age or Educational Experience." Unpublished doctoral dissertation, University of Minnesota, 1980.

Loevinger, J. *Ego Development: Conceptions and Theories.* San Francisco: Jossey-Bass, 1976.

Loevinger, J., and Wessler, R. *Measuring Ego Development.* Vol. I: *Construction and Use of a Sentence Completion Test.* San Francisco: Jossey-Bass, 1970.

Marcia, J. E. "Development and Validation of Ego Identity Status." *Journal of Personality and Social Psychology,* 1966, *3,* 551–558.

Mason, K. E. "The Effects of Developmental Instruction on the Development of Cognitive Complexity, Locus of Control, and Empathy in Beginning Counseling Graduate Students." Unpublished master's thesis, University of Maryland, 1978.

Mentkowski, M. "Using the Perry Scheme of Intellectual and Ethical Development as a College Outcomes Measure." Paper presented at the Perry Conference, St. Paul, Minnesota, June, 1981.

Meyer, P. "Intellectual Development: An Analysis of Religious Content." *Counseling Psychologist,* 1977, *6* (4), 47–50.

Mines, R. A. "The Mines-Jensen Interpersonal Relationship Inventory." Paper presented at the American College Personnel Association National Convention, Detroit, March, 1978.

Mines, R. A. "An Investigation of the Developmental Levels of Reflective Judgment and Associated Critical Thinking Skills in Young Adults." Unpublished doctoral dissertation, University of Iowa, 1980.

Mines, R. A. "Psychometric Aspects of the Reflective Judgment Interview Procedures." Paper presented at the meeting of the American College Personnel Association, Cincinnati, Ohio, May, 1981.

Mines, R. A., Gressard, C. F., and Daniels, H. "Evaluation in Student Services: A Metamodel." *Journal of College Student Personnel,* 1982, *23,* 195–201.

Moore, W. S. "The Measure of Intellectual Development: A Brief Review." Unpublished paper, Center for Applications of Developmental Instruction, University of Maryland–College Park, 1982.

Perry, W. G., Jr. *Forms of Intellectual and Ethical Development in the College Years.* New York: Holt, Rinehart and Winston, 1970.

Rest, J. R. "New Approaches in the Assessment of Moral Development." In T. Lickona (Ed.), *Moral Development and Behavior.* New York: Holt, Rinehart and Winston, 1976.

Rest, J. R. *Revised Manual for the Defining Issues Test.* Minneapolis: Moral Research Projects, University of Minnesota, 1979.

Rodgers, R. "Chickering's Vectors and Their Development in Women." Paper presented at the meeting of the American College Personnel Association, Detroit, Michigan, March, 1982.

Schroder, H., Driver, M., and Streufert, S. *Human Information Processing.* New York: Holt, Rinehart and Winston, 1967.

Shoff, S. P. "The Significance of Age, Sex, and Type of Education on the Development of Reasoning in Adults." Unpublished doctoral dissertation, University of Utah, 1979.

Slepitza, R. L. "The Validation of a Stage Model of Career Counseling." Unpublished master's thesis, University of Maryland, 1976.

Stephenson, B. W., and Hunt, C. "Intellectual and Ethical Development: A Dualistic Curriculum and Intervention for College Students." *Counseling Psychologist,* 1977, *6* (4), 39–42.

Strange, C. C. "Intellectual Development, Motive for Education, and Learning Styles During the College Years: A Comparison of Adult and Traditional Age College Students." Unpublished doctoral dissertation, University of Iowa, 1978.

Touchton, J. G., Wertheimer, L. C., Cornfeld, J. L., and Harrison, K. H. "Career Planning and Decision Making: A Developmental Approach to the Classroom." *Counseling Psychologist,* 1977, *6* (4), 42–47.

Viesar, K. G. "The Use of Cognitive Complexity, Characterological Type, Empathy, and Leaderless Group Discussion Measures as Evaluative Indices in the Selection of Orientation Advisors." Unpublished master's thesis, University of Maryland, 1978.

Welfel, E. R. "The Development of Reflective Judgment: Its Relationship to Year in College, Academic Major, and Satisfaction with Major Among College Students." Unpublished doctoral dissertation, University of Minnesota, 1979.

Welfel, E. R. "The Reflective Judgment Scores of College Students: A Closer Look." Paper presented at the meeting of the American College Personnel Association National Convention, Cincinnati, Ohio, April, 1981.

Wertheimer, L. C. "A New Model and Measure for Career Counseling: Incorporating Both Content and Processing Aspects of Career Concerns." Unpublished master's thesis, University of Maryland, 1976.

Wertheimer, L. C. "Relations Among Developmental Dimensions in Jane Loevinger's Model of Ego Development." Unpublished doctoral dissertation, University of Maryland, 1980.

Widick, C. "An Evaluation of Developmental Instruction in a University Setting." Unpublished doctoral dissertation, University of Minnesota, 1975.

Winston, R. B., Jr., Miller, T. K., and Prince, J. S. *Assessing Student Development.* Athens, Ga.: Student Development Associates, 1979.

Wirtz, P. G., and Magrath, D. S. "Creating Quality Programs." In M. J. Barr and L. A. Keating (Eds.), *New Directions for Student Services: Establishing Effective Programs,* no. 7. San Francisco: Jossey-Bass, 1979.

Wood, P. K. "The Analysis of the Structural Relationship Between Two Tests of Critical Thinking and Refelctive Judgment." Unpublished master's thesis, University of Iowa, 1980.

Robert A. Mines is an assistant professor of counseling psychology, School of Education, and senior staff psychologist, Counseling Services, at the University of Denver. Previously he was the acting coordinator of the Iowa Student Development Project at the University of Iowa. He has been involved in consulting and research on developmental stage and task issues in young adults.

Assessment can play an important role in student development programming efforts, and the student services professional must recognize when, how, and why assessment can be used in designing more effective student service programs.

Assessment in Student Development Programming: A Case Study

Kathleen J. Krone
Gary R. Hanson

This chapter describes a student development programming effort in a residence hall. What was key about this study was the major role that student assessment played in the program planning, delivery, and evaluation. The project highlights many of the problems, pitfalls, and rewards of doing developmental programming.

In the following sections, we will examine the context and background in which this study took place, identify eight stages of the project, and, at each stage, illustrate how the assessment of student development was incorporated into the overall project.

Background

The study was conducted in Jester Center, a megadorm at the University of Texas at Austin. Jester Center is a fourteen-story complex capable of holding approximately three thousand students. A variety of living options are available with the residence hall for students with spe-

G. R. Hanson (Ed.). *Measuring Student Development.* New Directions for Student Services, no. 20. San Francisco: Jossey-Bass, December 1982.

cial interests or desires, such as science and engineering, health sciences, twenty-four quiet hour, outdoor recreation, locked privacy, and freshman living experience, to name a few. When students are accepted to live at Jester Center, they are allowed to specify three living option preferences. Based on the kind of living options the student chooses, a variety of programming activities are available throughout the academic year.

Previous research conducted at the University of Texas had shown that the living options had a differential impact on academic performance (Barr, 1978; Yancey, 1979). The residence hall assistants and administrative staff also had conducted informal evaluations and noticed that certain living options seemed to influence the students in other ways. The freshman experience living option provides an opportunity for freshmen to live together in the same residence hall floor and to participate in a variety of activities that help them adjust to the university community. Over a several year period, the freshman experience living option had not only been very popular with the students but seemed to promote good academic performance and a sense of camaraderie. The staff also hypothesized that the freshman experience living option was having an impact on how students developed in other areas. The impetus for the current study arose out of these informal evaluations and a sense that something very important was happening. Since a systematic study had not been conducted, the administrative staff were not clear what aspect of the freshman experience living option contributed to the students' development. This was the context and rationale for the study.

Stage One: Laying the Groundwork

The first stage in conducting an experimental study of student development is primarily a political one. The idea for this project started with the senior author while she was employed in an administrative staff position within the Jester Center staff. She did not have direct responsibility for programming activities in the residence hall. Consequently, the idea for the study had to be discussed with a wide variety of people within the residence hall. The idea for the project itself was a simple one: How can we tell whether the students choosing the various living options are affected by the kinds of programming experiences provided by the staff? While the idea was a simple one, finding the answers would involve a complex activity that required the coordination and the cooperation of many other individuals.

The first step was to develop a political alliance with key residence hall staff. This was done by initiating a series of informal discussions with one particular residence hall assistant coordinator who, from past conversations, indicated an interest in participating in such a study. This initial phase of discussing the advantages and disadvantages of the proposed study is particularly important. It not only provides the instigator an opportunity to refine ideas but it also generates enthusiasm for the project and begins to establish important political ties that help the project gain acceptance. This stage also allows the project coordinator an opportunity to detect any negative reaction to the proposal and make the necessary adjustments before too much time, energy, and money are invested. Changes are easier to make at this point than later in the project. This stage is critical especially if the project coordinator is coming in from an external staff position or an administrative position removed from the direct delivery of service. In the case of this project, the senior author was not involved in the delivery of the developmental programming activities, and therefore had to spend time with those who were to make sure that she had support for the idea. This phase of project development takes what seems like an inordinate amount of time. Any time someone comes in from the outside, the staff who deliver the service are likely to be somewhat suspicious and unsure of the motives of the individual or team that wants to pursue the project. Far too often, however, this step is ignored or left out and the consequences are disastrous. Without a commitment of time and support from the front line staff, such a project is simply impossible. Call it public relations or networking or political alliance building — no matter what the term, it is an absolutely necessary step in any successful project. In terms of this particular project, several interested individuals agreed to participate if and when the project gained approval through the more formal administrative structure. Numerous ideas were discussed and the project coordinator had a much better idea about how to begin the next stage — formulating a specific plan.

Stage Two: Formulating a Plan

Before gaining approval to conduct the project, one must have a plan. At this stage, the input derived from the informal discussion with key friends and political alliances starts to pay off. While Stage One primarily involves a great deal of public relations and interaction with other people, the formulation of a research evaluation plan is a lonely task. One can use the ideas and the discussions from other individuals, but, at some point, one person must start to put together the pieces of the project. Questions such as the following must be answered:

- What aspect of the developmental program should be evaluated?
- What instruments are available to evaluate these elements?
- When trying to measure developmental growth, what should we look for?
- What kinds of control groups are needed to measure change?
- What kinds of compromises should be made between rigorous experimental design and political realities?
- Is it ethical to withhold developmental programming activities from one group while delivering such services to another?

The answers to these questions provide the critical elements in establishing an effective research design. Not all of the questions can be answered at once, and, in many ways, the answer to one question will directly influence what is feasible for another. For example, the cost of the assessment process directly influences the number of students who can be included in either an experimental or control group. Using a less expensive assessment process provides the opportunity to assess larger numbers of students, and subsequently, eliminates some of the randomness that is bound to be a part of any research design. However, the shorter, less expensive assessment instrument may not be sensitive enough to detect the developmental growth that is stimulated by a particular programming activity. Careful judgments must be made regarding the choice of an instrument because it influences the number of students who can be assessed and the chances of detecting any changes should they occur.

For this particular study, the development of the research design relied on the question of what impact the freshman experience living option had on the developmental status of students. Did students change in important ways due to their experiences with the freshman experience living option? If they changed, what kinds of experiences were related to that change? Which students changed? How much? These were all questions that the project coordinator raised at an early point in her deliberations. The primary concern was to answer the basic question of whether the nature of development of students involved in the freshman experience living option was different than the development of students choosing other living options in Jester Center. Because there were a wide variety of living option plans available, it seemed natural to compare the freshman experience living option with one or more other options. Not only was there interest in comparing the living options within Jester Center but the question arose whether the size and magnitude of the Jester Center complex in some way moderated the impact of the developmental programming activities. Did similar developmental programming activities in smaller, perhaps more cohesive, resident hall settings have an even greater impact on student development?

As the basic design of the study emerged, it was clear that the primary focus of the study would be to examine the freshman experience living option to determine what impact it had on the developmental growth of students over the period of one academic year. To determine whether growth had occurred for students participating in the freshman living option, a control group had to be identified and an appropriate selection instrument obtained. The question of appropriate control group seemed obvious: the traditional men's and women's residence halls on campus. These two groups were standard residence hall groups in that they represented a cross section of freshmen, sophomores, juniors, and seniors as well as many different educational majors and demographic backgrounds. At this point, the assessment process began to influence the design of the study. Decisions had to be made about what aspects of development were to be measured and the relative merits of possible assessment instruments. Since relatively large numbers of students live in each living option, it was important to find an assessment instrument that could be administered, scored, and interpreted with relative ease and at a low cost. As is often the case, funds were not yet available or approved for conducting the study. Often projects fail at this point because overambitious plans are developed which require more funds than most administrators are willing to commit. It was crucial, therefore, that a realistic approach be taken to the cost of the assessment process. As we looked for possible assessment instruments that would meet our two primary objectives of low cost and ease of administration, only one instrument seemed to satisfy both. We chose the Student Development Task Inventory developed by Winston, Miller, and Prince (1979). The Student Development Task Inventory was also selected because it measured three of Chickering's (1969) seven developmental vectors: Developing Autonomy, Developing Mature Interpersonal Relationships, and Developing Purpose. Each of these three developmental vectors were further broken down into three subtasks areas. These nine subcategories measured important developmental characteristics that were related to many of the programming activities traditionally provided in the freshman experience living option. The nine subcategories are: emotional autonomy, instrumental autonomy, interdependence, tolerance, relationships with peers, relationships with opposite sex, educational plans, career plans, and lifestyle plans.

The most difficult activity at this stage in the project planning process is to write down the basic elements of the evaluation project as a preliminary proposal. This requires that the ideas developed in Stage

One be combined with the more technical aspects of designing an appropriate research study. The preliminary proposal need not be elaborate but should contain certain key elements. A clear statement of the purpose that provides a rationale for why the study should be done is necessary. The general scope of the study, which includes the number of people involved, the basic research design, the assessment instrument, the time period over which this study will take place, anticipated cost, and the staff resources, should be included. The advantage of introducing a preliminary proposal is that it allows administrators an opportunity to adjust the plan to incorporate any special interests or ideas they may have. To illustrate the nature of a preliminary working proposal, Figure 1 presents the specific proposal for this project.

Stage Three: Selling the Plan

Selling the plan may be the most frustrating aspect of the entire project. Again, the political process of getting other people to buy the idea is the focus in this stage. Now that a more specific plan is available in written form, the plan must be moved up the ladder of administrative responsibility. Funds must be obtained, often a research committee must review the proposal, and key staff members must be willing to commit their time and effort to assure that the project is a success. Depending on the complexity of the organizational structure, one can begin to feel like a ping-pong ball during this stage. In many settings, evaluation projects like this one meet some resistance not only from the staff who might be implementing the program being evaluated but from other administrative staff members as well who may have a vested interest in maintaining the program as it is. These staff members may assume that changes are implied in the evaluation of the program and feel threatened.

On this project, another series of informal discussions were held with various staff members who were the resident assistants on those floors that were the focus of the study. Their cooperation and political support were absolutely crucial to getting the plan approved. In addition, a written presentation was made to the Jester Center Hall director. This written proposal contained all the major elements that were needed to give a clear idea of what the project would entail. Since the project was classified as a research project, the hall director, after reviewing the proposal, referred it to the residence hall research committee. The research committee consisted of a number of staff members from the residence hall who were asked to review all research proposals to evaluate

Figure 1. Preliminary Proposal

Project Proposal

I am requesting permission to administer the Student Development Task Inventory to a number of residents in Jester Center at the beginning of the fall semester and at the end of spring semester. In addition, I am requesting permission to work with several staff members to design specialized programs based on the results from the fall assessment.

Purpose

The purposes of the study are to:

1. Gather evaluative information concerning the freshman experience living option, and answer the question of whether the nature of development among students living there is different than those living elsewhere,

2. Gather evaluative information on men's and women's housing, and determine whether the nature of development among students living there is different than that of students in freshman experience living option,

3. Provide selected staff and a selected group of residents with needs assessment information to be used as a basis for forming individual and group development action plans,

4. Provide selected staff the experience of acting in the role of mentor to a limited number of residents,

5. Provide specified residents to opportunity to learn how to be responsible for their own development, thus allowing lifelong learning to occur.

Scope of the Study

Residents in the following areas would be surveyed:
Jester, Freshman Experience (four floors)
Jester, Men's Housing (one floor)
Jester, Women's Housing (one floor)
Women's Residence Halls (one hall)
Men's Residence Halls (one hall)

Residents on two of the freshman experience floors will be given the opportunity to work with a staff member (mentor) to develop personal action plans for the year.

The following internal staff members would be asked to contribute time to the study:

Assistant to the Director, Jester/Men's Residence Halls
Assistant Coordinator, Freshman Experience
Resident Assistants, Freshman Experience

If additional information is needed concerning the study, please let me know.

their merit and usefulness for the residence hall system. This particular aspect may not apply to other college and university residence hall systems.

One of the more frustrating aspects of this stage of project development is that of waiting for the response. A fair amount of time passed from when the project was originally submitted to the residence hall director to the time that it was formally approved by the research committee and the director of Housing. Individuals planning to do similar projects should count on large blocks of time when nothing seems to be happening. The project coordinator should realize that the review process allows administrators to "get used to the idea" of the project; the time it takes is usually well worth the wait. Once the research committee approved the basic concepts of the project and the residence hall director supported the intent, another level of commitment was pursued. Funds were not available to conduct research as part of the day-to-day residence hall budget. Consequently, the proposal needed the commitment and support of the director of Food and Housing, an individual who had multiple residence halls to supervise and coordinate. The proposal went forward and, again, large periods of time were spent waiting to address his questions and concerns — and waiting for a formal decision. As the project proposal progressed from one level of administration to the next, a particularly good selling point of the proposal was the assessment instrument, the Student Development Task Inventory. While a description of the instrument and its psychometric qualities were not included in the proposal itself, the usefulness of the instrument in measuring developmental growth was communicated in an informal manner at each step. This instrument lent a great deal of credibility to the study. Submitting a proposal with an assessment process that was not well documented or researched may have endangered the approval process for the project.

Another key element in this third stage is the importance of developing a sense of when to wait for a response and when to push for a decision. The final draft of this particular project proposal was formally submitted near the beginning of the spring semester and the review process took most of the semester. The project coordinator knew that, in order to train the residence hall staff to conduct the project, at least two weeks would be required before the end of the semester. Since formal approval for the project had not yet been given at this point, the project coordinator approached the residence hall director and the director of Food and Housing to obtain a final decision. Approval was granted and funds were available to conduct the study during the fall and spring semester of the next year.

Stage Four: Prepreparation

To successfully complete an evaluation project, a wide variety of prepreparation activities must occur. For this project, the residence hall assistants (RAs) had to be trained in the use of the Student Development Task Inventory. By this time, the residence hall assistants were committed to the project. The groundwork laid in Stage One and Stage Three had paid off. The basic idea did not have to be sold to the residence hall staff at this point. However, these individuals did require some training in the use of the assessment instrument. While most of the key staff had reviewed the Chickering theory of college student development as part of their graduate training programs, or as part of the resident assistance class, a brief review was included at the end of the spring semester to reacquaint them with the basic tenets of the theory. In addition, each staff member was asked to take the Student Development Task Inventory, to score their own assessment results, and to create a developmental plan for the summer. Assistance was provided to help them understand and interpret the results. By giving the staff practice in using the assessment instrument, they could see how the instrument might be used with residents in the coming year. Students would be given the instrument in September and the residence hall assistants would help them interpret the results; then, an individualized developmental programming plan was to be developed in consultation with the residence hall assistant for that living option.

The goal at this stage is to identify all those activities that must be done before the project begins. Staff members must become familiar with the assessment process; taking and scoring the instrument is a good way to accomplish this. By taking the instrument themselves, the staff can gain a sense of the process and can anticipate the kinds of questions or the problems that students might encounter. Familiarity with the assessment process can also increase the enthusiasm for the project.

Stage 5: Adjustment Stage

Every developmental programming activity and student development assessment project requires a stage of adjustment—a time to refine the project plans in light of practical realities. One of the advantages of identifying all the project activities in the previous prepreparation stage is that each required step can be evaluated with respect to its feasibility. Asking whether each step can, in fact, be done and then making the necessary plans to accomplish them often forces the project coordinator to add, drop, or modify some of the original project tasks. The original plan for this study included a step in which the residence hall assistants met with each student after the pre-assessment stage and helped them develop an individualized developmental plan. With several hundred students participating in the study, the feasibility of working with that many students on an individual basis seemed impossible. While the idea had considerable merit, the practical limitations of staff, time, and money forced the project coordinators to redesign this aspect of the project. Group developmental programming activities were substituted for individualized plans.

Stage Six: Pre-Assessment

In order to measure student development, it is necessary to make an assessment prior to the delivery of any student service program. The very nature of development implies that development has a starting point or initial status from which future growth or development will take place. When trying to assesss both the magnitude and direction of change that can be attributed to particular programming activities, it is critical that appropriate control groups be established and administered the same pre-assessment instrument. In the case of this project, four separate floors of the freshmen experience living option were given the Student Development Task Inventory; one men's floor and one women's floor in Jester were given the same instrument at approximately the same point in time. As students came back for the fall semester, they were given the option to self-select a living option. A more rigorous design may have been possible if students could have been randomly assigned to one of the four living options. However, the administrative decision to keep the same set of procedures from one year to the next prevailed. As a result, the pre-assessment is even more important when randomized groups are not possible, since it helps establish whether group differences existed before the developmental programming activities were implemented.

For this study, six floors of Jester Center were involved in the study, each floor containing ninety-two residents. Four floors (two male and two female) comprised the freshman experience living option. One floor of male traditional housing and one floor of female traditional housing were used as a control group. Students were asked to voluntarily participate in the study and were encouraged to complete the assessment instrument during an evening residence hall meeting. Of the 552 possible residents, only 353 (64 percent) actually completed the pre-assessment instrument. The fact that not all students participated created the possibility of a potential bias in the study results. That similar proportions of students from the freshman living experience and the two control group floors was obtained somewhat reduced the possibility of bias. After completing the Student Development Task Inventory, the students living in the freshman experience living option were asked to score their questionnaire and were given an interpretive brochure that helped them understand the meaning of their scores. Students in the control group did not score their own questionnaires and thus were not involved in the self-assessment process. This assessment occurred during the month of September, and, in the month that followed, the freshman experience residence hall assistants were asked to continue programming as they had in the past and also to implement special developmental programs designed by the project coordinator in conjunction with the residence hall coordinator for the freshmen experience floors. The control group residence hall assistants were simply asked to do the traditional educational programming.

Stage Seven: Delivering the Program

Both the control group and the freshman experience living option group were required to conduct a variety of educational programming activities over the course of the fall and spring semesters at the University of Texas. These programming activities generally emphasized social programming. For example, parties, intramural sports activities, and social functions conducted within residence hall floor systems were typically done by all the residence hall floors. For purposes of this project, however, three developmental programming activities were included for the freshman experience living option floors. One section of the special programming involved the presentation by the orientation office of a program designed to assist students in adjusting to university life and in dealing with issues concerning separation from parents. A two-part program, sponsored by the Career Choice and Information Center in conjunction with the freshman experience residence hall assistants, focused on values, skill identification processes, and career planning. These three programs comprised the intentional developmental programming dimension of this project. The two control groups did not receive these special developmental programming activities. The intent was to see whether these three programs had a significant impact on the developmental progress of students who participated in them as compared with students who did not.

As with many developmental programming activities, the manner in which these programs were developed raised many questions.

Some of the most difficult were: What was the developmental program? Did various components of the overall programming activities have a differential impact on some students and not others? To what can the observed impact be attributed? To answer these kinds of questions requires that very detailed records be maintained about who participated in what kinds of activities and when. To determine whether each part of the program contributed to the developmental growth of students, it would have been necessary to readminister the Student Development Task Inventory to each student following each programming activity. This was not feasible, given the high cost and excessive administrative record keeping. Consequently, it was decided to examine the overall impact of the three developmental programming activities as a whole. Once the program is delivered, a second assessment process must take place.

Stage Eight: Post-Assessment

Just as the first assessment provided a benchmark or starting point from which to judge whether developmental progress had been made, the second assessment is also important in that it provides a termination point for purposes of comparison. The most difficult task at this stage is to get students to retake the assessment instrument. After all the students in the freshman experience living option completed the three components of the developmental programming activities, the entire group of students were asked to meet in the evening once again and to retake the Student Development Task Inventory. At this time, both the freshman experience living option students and the control group students were asked to score their assessment instruments and received interpretive information and a brief explanation of what their scores meant.

Another important aspect of this stage is the manipulation of the data that occurs beyond the original scoring. The data must be coded, entered into a computer readable format and analyzed. Special care must be taken to ensure that the two sets of scores (pre- and post-) are available from the same individual for both assessments. The first score indicates where the student started from; the second score where the student ended. These two sets of scores give an indication of both the direction of the developmental change and the magnitude. It is not unusual that at least some of the students will digress in their development and score lower after developmental programming activities than before. However, most students will show increased levels of development. The question then becomes whether students receiving the developmental programming experiences changed more than those who did not. To determine this, it is necessary to compare how the experimental and control groups scored on the pre-assessment, identify the direction and the magnitude of the change for both groups, and determine whether there are group differences at the posttest assessment. Often, sophisticated and complicated statistical techniques are required to show whether or not any change occurred for either group and whether the nature of that change was different. The analysis cannot begin without carefully considering the nature of the audience who will eventually receive the results. It does very little good to conduct complicated statistical analyses if the intended audience has little or no understanding of what those statistical tests mean. Thus, perhaps the most important stage is showing how students change.

Stage Nine: Showing that Students Develop

The last stage of a developmental assessment project requires a careful identification of who should get the results and for what purposes. After spending nearly nine months conducting this study, it was more important than ever that time be set aside to think about how best to report the results. The questions we asked at this point were: Who would like to see the results of our project? Who has to see them? Who is most likely to benefit from positive results? or be threatened by negative results? What is the statistical sophistication of the people most likely to read or receive the report of the study? How can we best report the results in clear, concise, and understandable fashion?

As we reviewed the preliminary data analyses for this particular project, we were struck by how strong an impact developmental programming seemed to have on the students who lived in the freshman experience living option when compared to the control groups. To analyze the data, mean differences between the freshman experience living option and the control groups pre-assessment scores were tested using a simple one-way analysis of variance. Seven of the nine subcategory scores of the Student Development Task Inventory showed no initial difference, but two of them did. Consequently, the posttest scores were compared, using analysis of covariance with the pretest scores as a covariant. This particular analysis took into consideration the preassessment score differences that existed in the groups initially formed for this study. As statisticians and researchers, we knew we had highly significant results. Our interpretation of the data was that the developmental programming activities made a very strong impact on the developmental status of students. But F-ratios, covariants, matrices, and adjusted mean differences were not going to have much meaning to most of our audience. We needed to figure out a better way to make the data understandable. We finally decided to prepare one simple chart which showed the change in score as a percentage of the original score value. These percentage changes were plotted on a bar graph, taking into consideration the direction of the change. For each of the nine scales, we plotted the percentage change in scores for the Freshman Experience Living Option and the control groups. The data are reproduced in Figure 2 to show how effective this graphic representation was. It is immediately evident from the graph that the freshman experience students changed in a positive way in several dimensions that the control group did not and that these changes appear to be directly related to the programming efforts.

Figure 2. Percent Change in SDTI Subscale Scores from Pre-Test to Post-Test by Group

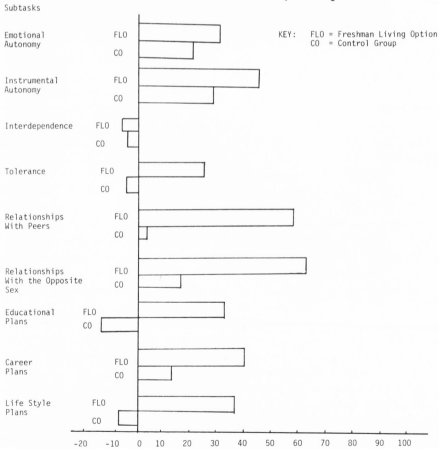

As we looked at the results of this study, we felt sure that everybody would be impressed with our efforts and that the value of the developmental programming activities would be readily apparent. Generally speaking the results were easily understood by those who reviewed them. However, the results were disseminated in the last weeks of the semester, and much of their impact was lost. With students leaving for the summer and the usual turnover in residence hall assistant staff, many of the informal techniques for communicating the results were not available for this study. The data showed solid justification for the developmental programming activities that were conducted, but a variety of other factors, as is often the case, intervened to minimize the overall impact of the study.

Evaluating the Project

The focus of the program described in this chapter was to evaluate a specific developmental programming experience in a large residence hall. The assessment process played an important role at several key stages throughout the study. We will identify the ways in which good assessment practices were taken advantage of, and ways in which we could have made even better use of assessment. Sometimes the assessment process was intuitively employed; at other times it was planned in detail. Once the idea of comparing the nature and magnitude of developmental growth in student living in one kind of residence hall setting with students living in a different setting was established, the assessment process began to play an important role in Stage Two. An instrument had to be selected that was easy to score and inexpensive. These two limitations rather quickly narrowed our choice to one available instrument. But once this instrument was selected, it began to have an influence on other aspects of the research design. Because the assessment instrument was based on Chickering's theory of student development, decisions could be made about what aspects of student development should be assessed, what developmental programming activities should be planned, and what types of changes might possibly occur. In most studies, the assessment process will play an important role in the overall design of the study. We also used the assessment instrument to promote and sell the idea of the project to various administrative staff and participants. The assessment instrument lent credibility to the project by providing a conceptual base on student development. Individuals in the residence hall setting recognized the theory and were at least somewhat familiar with the instrument itself. Approval of the project seemed to be easier and enthusiasm gained momentum because people could more easily conceptualize what might take place. Some fears and anxieties about program evaluation were also reduced because a well-tested instrument was being used in place of poorly-documented instruments or informal assessment techniques. The assessment instrument also played a key role in the prepreparation stage. We used the instrument to not only train the residence hall assistants in how to administer, score, and interpret the Student Development Task Inventory, but we also felt that the project participants gained a greater self-understanding as a result of completing the instrument.

Another way in which the assessment process was used in the project was to include the administration of the Student Development Task Inventory as part of the treatment intervention that was given to the freshman experience students. Not only did the students take and score their assessment results but they were also given a group interpretation. Our original intent was to design individual developmental learning opportunities, but the magnitude of the project and the detailed record keeping necessary to conduct that part of the project was more than our resources allowed. Nevertheless, the assessment process allowed us to encourage students to think about themselves in developmental terms. The design of our study did not allow us to determine whether students were then more receptive to the developmental programming activities that occurred. Given the magnitude of the change for freshman experience students compared to traditional students, we could not help but wonder if the assessment instrument was important in this way. Finally, the assessment process allowed us to determine whether any change took place or not. With pretests and posttests available, we could compare scores for students who lived in one or the other living options. As a result of the postassessment analysis, we could make evaluative judgments about the value of student development programming activities. Without the assessment results, we could have only guessed whether our programming activities had an impact on the students. We certainly would not have been able to recognize the magnitude of the changes.

Obviously, if we had the opportunity to conduct the project again, we would make a number of changes in procedure. The most difficult part of the project was to get the students to participate in the assessment process. From September to April, only about 20 percent of the students available completed both the pre- and postassessment instruments. Because of attrition, we were unable to determine whether this small subgroup, representing 20 percent of the total number of students on the living option floors, changed in ways that were significantly different from the general student population on those floors. We undoubtedly have a considerable degree of bias in our results, but we do not know the nature of that bias. Perhaps the students who willingly participate in such projects are simply more sensitive to the impact of the developmental programming activities. With an opportunity to do the study again, efforts could be made to collect data from a larger portion of the students in the various living options. Another factor beyond our control was that the students who did not live in the freshman experience options dropped out of the University and, hence, left the residence hall at a much larger rate than the students in the freshman experience halls. Perhaps the lack of student development or the negative change in the developmental status of some students on the control group floors would have been even greater had these students not dropped out.

One of the most important things we learned from conducting this study was that other factors played a significant role in how much attention is given to the final results. When other competing activities — whether they are administrative detail, staff turnover, or bad timing — interfere, is it very difficult to get people to pay attention to even very significant findings. A great deal of time, effort, and money was spent in the planning, delivery, and analysis stages of this study. With longitudinal designs like this one, it is always difficult to maintain the enthusiasm and the energy to promote the findings to the right people once the project is over. This is a critical stage that must be attended to with all the energy of the previous stages. Most often, however, it is not. If we had the opportunity to conduct the study one more time, we would allow more time before the end of the school year to analyze and report our data.

Summary

Assessment can play a variety of roles in an evaluation design concerned with the developmental growth of students. Assessment can be used to refine the research design, to sell the idea to administrative staff and project participants, as part of the treatment intervention, and to provide a benchmark for determining whether any student growth occurred or not. Other projects will reveal additional ways that assessment can facilitate the student developmental programming experience. We must continue looking for new ways to include the assessment activity as an integral part of our programming activities. When assessment is included, we have greater confidence that what we do has an impact.

References

Barr, M. J. "A Summary of Academic Performance for Freshmen Jester Center Residents by Living Option and Sex: Fall, 1978." In *Office of the Dean of Students Office Research Report.* Austin: M. J. Barr, University of Texas, 1978.

Chickering, A. *Education and Identity.* San Francisco: Jossey-Bass, 1969.

Winston, R. B., Miller, T. K., and Prince, J. S. *Assessing Student Development.* Athens, Ga.: Student Development Associates, 1979.

Yancey, B. D. "Demographic Profile of Spring 1979 Residents of University Housing." In *Office of the Dean of Students Office Research Report.* Austin: B. D. Yancey, University of Texas, 1979.

Kathleen J. Krone is currently a doctoral candidate in organizational/interpersonal communication at the University of Texas at Austin. She is assistant instructor in the Department of Communication and research associate in the Student Life Studies unit of the Office of the Dean of Students. Throughout the implementation of this project, she was an administrative staff member at Jester Center at the University of Texas.

Gary R. Hanson is assistant dean of students at the University of Texas at Austin and is responsible for the Student Life Studies unit of the Office of the Dean of Students.

The assessment of student development is at an exciting
period in its history. With a solid theoretical foundation,
the assessment process can be examined for ways to make it
more viable for those who work directly with students.

Concluding Remarks
and Additional Resources

Gary R. Hanson

Over the last ten years, student affairs professionals have watched with
excitement the explosion of interest in the theoretical writings on human
development. We no longer have to grope for a way to understand students. Numerous theories and sophisticated conceptual models help us
understand how and when students change. Also, a good deal has been
written about designing and implementing programs, especially those
programs which stimulate students to change in important ways (Barr
and Keating, 1979; Moore and Delworth, 1976). At the same time, a
large and growing literature urges that we evaluate what we do (Hanson, 1978; Kuh, 1979; Mines, Gressard, and Daniels, 1982). These
evaluation methods are designed to help us understand what elements of
our programming efforts influence student development, but we almost
never make the final connection between program elements and student
growth. The major thesis of this entire volume has been that the assessment of student development is a critical link in that process, but a very
weak one. We have not documented that students change as a result of

G. R. Hanson (Ed.). *Measuring Student Development.* New Directions
for Student Services, no. 20. San Francisco: Jossey-Bass, December 1982.

our programming efforts because we have limited assessment instruments. Our instruments are crude, cumbersome, expensive, difficult to administer, even more difficult to score, and almost impossible to communicate to others once we have the data. Sound like a dismal state of affairs? Not necessarily.

In Chapter One, Theodore Miller pointed out that we have the philosophy, the theory, the rationale, and the motivation to seek new horizons in the assessment of student development. This rich conceptual background gives us much to think about and suggests important areas in which we should be developing new assessment instruments. Karen Kitchener, in Chapter Two, takes a look at our developmental theories and identifies two major domains that we must measure if we are to understand how students develop throughout their college career. Before we can help students, we need to understand how they think and reason. Thus, the social-cognitive developmental process is one that we need to develop good assessment instruments for. Kitchener also points out that we must assess and measure student developmental tasks. These tasks involve developing new attitudes, roles, and skills. The manner in which students think and the developmental tasks they must encounter during college are not independent or unrelated events. To avoid the developmental double bind that students encounter when they are faced with difficult developmental tasks that require more complex decision making than they have learned, student affairs professionals must develop new kinds of programs and services. To do that, however, requires an accurate assessment of the developmental status of students in terms of the tasks they have accomplished as well as an accurate assessment of the social-cognitive thinking processes they use. Hanson identifies the barriers to an effective assessment program in Chapter Three. None of these barriers is insurmountable, but it requires a concentrated effort to find solutions. Some of the barriers are political and will require astute administrators to make sure that the developmental perspective continues to be an important goal of higher education. Other barriers are psychometric and involve complex measurement issues. Many of these barriers will not be resolved until we have student affairs professionals with more extensive training in the field of measurement and evaluation. Finding solutions to any of the barriers mentioned by Hanson requires that long-range planning be implemented with the thought of including the developmental assessment process at every level of the design and delivery of student service programs. Likewise, solutions to the problems we now face will require that experimental studies like the one described by Krone and Hanson in this volume will help us relate the effects of developmental programming to student growth and development. Without more of these studies, we will never find out what aspects of our programming activities really influence the manner and magnitude of student development.

A great deal of this volume on the assessment of student development has been devoted to taking a critical look at our current state of affairs. The authors have pointed out that much remains to be done. We are at a very early stage in our knowledge and our procedures for assessing developmental status of students. However, we can look to some very promising possibilities for new directions that our assessment of student development may take in the future.

Looking to the Future

The assessment instruments and methods available today form a solid foundation for some very exciting possibilities. A growing number of researchers and practitioners are actively pursuing the refinement of our student development assessment instruments. Over the next five to ten years, we can expect to see the following kinds of advancements in our assessment of student development. First, the amount of data we collect from students will be reduced dramatically. Both time consuming interviews and cumbersome paper-and-pencil procedures will become the dinosaurs of the student development profession. Our student development assessment instruments of the future will not only be shorter but, at the same time, they will measure more complex behavior and thought processes. The long, time-consuming assessment procedures that now yield simple developmental stage scores will be discontinued in favor of shorter instruments that provide developmental profiles showing the status of a given student along many important dimensions of development. One of the consequences of making the assessment instrument shorter, but accessing more complex dimensions of student development, is that the cost of assessments will be reduced. This will make it much more practical to provide developmental assessment opportunities to large numbers of students.

In the future, student development assessment instruments will become more diagnostic and prescriptive in nature. As we collect more assessment data, relationships between the student services programs we deliver and the manner and timing of how students change will be better established. In the future, we should be able to use assessment data to design programs for students with similar developmental needs. We should also be able to identify what kinds of program experiences lead to changes in student autonomy, the development of identity, and the manner in which students reason and think. At first, student affairs professionals may need to work very closely with the students to help them interpret and understand the assessment data. At some distant point in time, however, the instruments may be refined to the point of self-diagnosis. Students need to be involved in the assessment process and they need to actively engage in the kinds of activities that challenge them to grow and mature in educationally important ways.

One of the greatest impacts on the refinement of the student development assessment process will be the incorporation of computer-assisted assessment. Computer systems now exist that could be used to administer the assessment process, synthesize the results, provide narrative reports back to the students immediately, store the data in part of a college or university's management information system, as well as provide prescriptive opportunities that would facilitate student development. The college student of the future may well sit at home at a computer terminal, apply to college, complete a battery of assessment instruments, and, as a result, receive a broad list of educational opportunities, perhaps spread throughout the United States, that would be available at a very reasonable cost. The computer terminal could also be used to generate a developmental transcript that would monitor as well as help the student plan additional developmental activities. Upon the student's request, these developmental transcripts could be sent to future employers who would seek students that have various accomplishments and important developmental dimensions. While the student would have a very direct involvement in designing and participating in a wide variety of educational activities, our educational institutions of the future would also have the opportunity to use data in a management information system to evaluate, modify, and improve various components of the educational activities they provide for students. While this scenario may seem radical, improbable, and perhaps even undesirable by many, the fact remains that the technology is available to accomplish it. What remains to be done requires continued effort to conceptualize our student development theory, to further refine our assessment process, and most importantly, to study the link between student development and its antecedent causes. As Miller pointed out, assessment provides the glue that holds the developmental process together. Without the proper application of our developmental glue, our student service programs are likely to fall apart.

References

Barr, M. J., and Keating, L. A. *New Directions for Student Services: Establishing Effective Programs,* no. 7. San Francisco: Jossey-Bass, 1979.

Hanson, G. R. (Ed.). *New Directions for Student Services: Evaluating Program Effectiveness,* no. 1. San Francisco: Jossey-Bass, 1978.

Kuh, G. D. (Ed.). *Evaluation in Student Affairs.* Cincinnati, Ohio: American College Personnel Association, 1979.

Mines, R. A., Gressard, C. F., and Daniels, H. "Evaluation in the Student Services: A Metamodel." *Journal of College Student Personnel,* 1982, *23* (3), 195–201.

Moore, M., and Delworth, U. *Training Manual for Student Service Program Development.* Boulder, Colo.: Western Interstate Commission for Higher Education, 1976.

Additional References

The references cited here are provided for the interested reader who wishes to learn more about the assessment of student development. I did not intend that the list represent an exhaustive bibliography of all the important references that should be read; rather I merely wanted to indicate a selection of basic references I have found useful over the years. A range of readings is provided for the graduate student and new professional with limited training in measurement and evaluation and also for the technically sophisticated researcher. I undoubtedly omitted some material which you have found helpful in your work and I simply ask that you draw those references to the attention of your colleagues in the same manner I have done in this section.

Baird, L. L. (Ed.). *New Directions for Community Colleges: Assessing Student Academic and Social Progress,* no. 18. San Francisco: Jossey-Bass, 1977.

The volume provides a good overview of the role assessment should play in higher education, particularly the community college system. A number of good chapters are included that examine a broad range of college outcomes, many of which are developmental in nature.

Hanson, G. R., and Lenning, O. T. "Evaluating Student Development Programs." In G. Kuh (Ed.), *Evaluation in Student Affairs.* Cincinnati, Ohio: ACPA Media Publication No. 26, 1979.

This chapter describes the use of student development assessment data for the purpose of program evaluation. Many of the issues and problems of conducting good evaluation of student service programs that emphasize growth and development are highlighted.

Lenning, O. T. "Assessment and Evaluation." In U. Delworth, G. R. Hanson and Associates (Eds.), *Student Services: A Handbook for the Profession.* San Francisco: Jossey-Bass, 1980.

The distinction between evaluation and assessment is made in this chapter. The many uses of assessment are described and guidelines are provided for how to evaluate the usefulness of various assessment instruments.

Fried, J. *New Directions for Student Services: Education for Student Development,* no. 15. San Francisco: Jossey-Bass, 1981.

Though this volume of the *New Directions for Student Services* series is not oriented directly to the assessment of student development, it is an important reference work for those readers who want to apply the results of assessment in the academic classroom. There are a number of good "how-to" chapters which point out how assessment results can be used to design curricula, to play a role in the consultation process, and to form the basis of the evaluation of developmental instruction.

Brown, R. D., and DeCoster, D. A. (Eds.). *New Directions for Student Services: Mentoring-Transcript Systems for Promoting Student Growth,* no. 19. San Francisco: Jossey-Bass, 1982.

This volume provides a conceptual model of the developmental mentoring-transcript process in which assessing the developmental status of students is a critical element of the model. The College Student Development Self-Assessment Inventory, an informal but very useful instrument, is also introduced.

Miller, T. K., and Prince, J. S. *The Future of Student Affairs.* San Francisco: Jossey-Bass, 1976.

Chapter Three in this book is titled, "Assessing Individual Growth" and provides a good starting point for how and why student affairs professionals should be interested in assessing student growth. A rationale for the assessment of student development is provided. Guidelines for establishing a self-assessment program are outlined, and a practical example is detailed.

Loevinger, J. *Ego Development: Conceptions and Theories.* San Francisco: Jossey-Bass, 1976.

This book represents a classic in the field and should be required reading by everyone. Chapter Eight deals with the issues in defining stages and types of development and presents a clear discussion of the issues from a philosophical point of view. Student affairs professionals interested in becoming well versed in the design, development, and use of student development measures should become intimately familiar with Chapter Nine titled, "Issues and Strategies of Measurement."

Messick, S. "Constructs and Their Vicissitudes in Educational and Psychological Measurement." *Psychological Bulletin,* 1981, *89* (3), 575–588.

This article is written for the more sophisticated measurement specialist but is required reading for anyone trying to make sense out of the relationship between an assessment model or procedure and the theoretical construct that is being assessed. Anyone trying to develop an assessment instrument based on a particular theory should definitely read this article several times.

Winston, R. B., Miller, T. K., Hackney, S. T., Hodges, J. L., Polkosnik, M. C., Robinson, J. A., and Russo, B. A. "Assessing Student Development: A Developmental Approach." *Journal of College Student Personnel,* 1981, *22* (5), 429–435.

This article describes the development and testing of the Student Development Task Inventory-2, an inventory which assesses three of Chickering's developmental vectors. Each developmental task — developing autonomy, developing purpose, and developing mature interpersonal relationships — is assessed using three subtask measures. Both reliability and selected validity data are reported to support the usefulness of the instrument.

Rest, J. R. "New Approaches in the Assessment of Moral Development." In T. Lickona (Ed.), *Moral Development and Behavior.* New York: Holt, Rinehart and Winston, 1976.

This chapter describes the problems of measuring developmental stages. Rest questions the traditional methods of scoring and interpreting developmental measures and suggests many new ways of approaching the measurement of human development.

Pfeiffer, J., Heslin, R., and Jones, J. *Instrumentation in Human Relations Training.* San Diego, Calif.: University Associates, 1976.

This book offers a wide collection of instruments that measure various dimensions of development. Student affairs professionals responsible for designing new student services, modifying old ones, or evaluating current programs will find this book a tremendous help. The reader should be cautioned that the instruments are in various stages of validation and must be chosen with care.

Morrill, W., and Hurst, J. (Eds.). *Dimensions of Interventions for Student Development.* New York: Wiley, 1980.

This book deals less with the issues of assessment and measurement but, instead, outlines a model for designing intervention strategies and student service program delivery methods. Consequently, excellent suggestions are provided for incorporating assessment data into the program development process.

Student Development Assessment Instruments

The purpose of this section is to introduce the reader to a few instruments that are commonly used to assess various dimensions of student development. Not all of the instruments are of the same quality and may vary in the amount of supporting validity data available. My intent was not to provide an exhaustive list of possible instruments. (If you are instrument hunting, I suggest you refer to the *Buros Mental Measurement Yearbook* or the Pfeiffer, Heslin, and Jones (1976) reference cited earlier.) Rather, the instruments listed here are available, show promise of being useful, and measure dimensions of college student development that seem to be important. I have tried to include a mix of instruments that represent sophisticated research instruments and that require expert raters and a considerable amount of data collection effort as well as paper and pencil instruments which are simple, easy-to-use, and inexpensive.

College Student Development Self-Assessment Instrument. This inventory was developed as part of the developmental mentoring-transcript project at the University of Nebraska, Lincoln, and is reported in Brown and DeCoster (1982). The instrument consists of fifty-six different dimensions clustered in six major areas of personal development. Students are asked to anser three questions related to each item: (1) What is your proficiency or knowledge level? (2) How satisfied are you with your ability in this area? and (3) Would you like to talk about this topic to either get a better idea of your skills or find out what you might improve? The six major clusters include:

- Personal identity and life style
- Multicultural awareness
- Interpersonal skills and relationships
- Academic skills and intellectual competencies
- Aesthetic awareness
- Health, physical fitness, and recreation.

Additional information regarding this assessment instrument may be obtained from the Developmental Mentoring Transcript Clearinghouse, University of Nebraska, Lincoln.

Defining Issues Test (DIT). This instrument was reviewed by Mines (1982) in an earlier chapter of this volume. The DIT was designed to assess moral development from Kohlberg's cognitive stage perspective and is available in both a long and a short form. The instrument contains an instruction page and three or six stories that represent various moral dilemmas. Students mark their responses on an answer sheet which can be either hand scored or computer scored. The scoring system provides a profile of the percentage stage level marked by the students.

To obtain copies of the manual and instrument, contact Dr. James Rest, Minnesota Moral Research Projects, 330 Barton Hall, University of Minnesota, Minneapolis, Minnesota 55455.

The Measurement of Intellectual Development. The measurement of intellectual development (MID) was designed to assess three specific cognitive stage level domains identified by Perry's theory (1969). The instrument consists of three essays which each take about fifteen minutes to complete. The essays are used to assess the level of cognitive development with respect to decision making, careers, and classroom learning. To score the MID, expert raters assigned a three-digit rating which represents a stable position rating as well as two possible transitional steps between each stable position. The psychometric data supporting this instrument are reviewed by Mines (1982). Further information regarding the instrument can be obtained by writing to the Center for the Application of Developmental Instruction, University of Maryland, 9504 52 Avenue, College Park, Maryland 20740.

Reflective Judgment Interview (RJI). The purpose of the reflective judgment interview instrument is to provide a description of the subjects' intellectual stage functioning according to the Perry model. The RJI is used to collect data via an hour-long interview in which one of four dilemmas is verbally presented as the student follows along on an identical written copy. A tape recording is made of the student's responses and transcribed and rated by certified judges. A single stage score is obtained by averaging the ratings across raters and dilemmas. Additional information about the RJI can be obtained from Dr. Karen Kitchener at CGB 112, School of Education, University of Denver, Denver, CO 80208.

Student Development Task Inventory-2. The student development task inventory-2 (SDTI-2) assesses three of Chickering's (1969) vectors of student development: developing autonomy, developing purpose, and freeing interpersonal relationships. Students respond to 140 items which are marked true or false and scored on three subtasks within each of the three major developmental domains. The SDTI-2 can be administered individually or in groups and takes about twenty to thirty minutes to complete. The answer sheets can be self-scored by the students. Individuals interested in scoring the SDTI-2 using a computer should contact Student Development Associates. The scoring costs are substantially lower than other available instruments, making the SDTI-2 a popular instrument for larger scale studies. Additional information regarding the SDTI-2 is available by writing to: Student Development Associates, Inc., 110 Crestwood Drive, Athens, GA 30605, or Consulting Pyschologists Press, 577 College Avenue, Palo Alto, CA 94306.

*Gary R. Hanson is assistant dean of students
at the University of Texas at Austin.*

Index

STATEMENT OF OWNERSHIP, MANAGEMENT, AND CIRCULATION
(Required by 39 U.S.C. 3685)

1. Title of Publication: New Directions for Student Services. A. Publication number: USPS 449-070. 2. Date of filing: September 30, 1982. 3. Frequency of issue: quarterly. A. Number of issues published annually: four. B. Annual subscription price: $35 institutions; $21 individuals. 4. Location of known office of publication: 433 California Street, San Francisco (San Francisco County), California 94104. 5. Location of the headquarters or general business offices of the publishers: 433 California Street, San Francisco (San Francisco County), California 94104. 6. Names and addresses of publisher, editor, and managing editor: publisher—Jossey-Bass Inc., Publishers, 433 California Street, San Francisco, California 94104; editor—Ursula Delworth, Gary R. Hanson, University of Iowa, Counseling Center, Iowa City, Iowa 52242; managing editor—Allen Jossey-Bass, 433 California Street, San Francisco, California 94104. 7. Owner: Jossey-Bass Inc., Publishers, 433 California Street, San Francisco, California 94104. 8. Known bondholders, mortgages, and other security holders owning or holding 1 percent or more of total amount of bonds, mortgages, or other securities: same as No. 7. 10. Extent and nature of circulation: (Note: first number indicates the average number of copies of each issue during the preceding twelve months; the second number indicates the actual number of copies published nearest to filing date.) A. Total number of copies printed (net press run): 2776, 2695. B. Paid circulation, 1) Sales through dealers and carriers, street vendors, and counter sales: 85, 40. 2) Mail subscriptions: 781, 758. C. Total paid circulation: 866, 998. D. Free distribution by mail, carrier, or other means (samples, complimentary, and other free copies): 125, 125. E. Total distribution (sum of C and D): 991, 923. F. Copies not distributed, 1) Office use, left over, unaccounted, spoiled after printing: 1785, 1772. 2) Returns from news agents: 0, 0. G. Total (sum of E, F1, and 2—should equal net press run shown in A): 2776, 2695.

I certify that the statements made by me above are correct and complete.

JOHN R. WARD
Vice-President